GUIDE TO
Marine Mammals & Turtles of the U.S. Atlantic & Gulf of Mexico

Written by Kate Wynne & Malia Schwartz
Illustrated by Garth Mix

Alaska Sea Grant
University of Alaska Fairbanks
Fairbanks, AK 99775-5040
(888) 789-0090 • Fax (907) 474-6285
Price: $25.00

Kate Wynne

Since 1981, Kate Wynne has been involved in assessing marine mammal populations and their interactions with commercial fisheries. She has surveyed, captured, and necropsied more than a dozen species of marine mammals in the Atlantic and Pacific, including cetaceans, pinnipeds, and sea otters. She has been a marine mammal observer, designed and coordinated marine mammal observer programs, and continues to train fishery observers in marine mammal identification. She studied harbor seals and marine mammal interactions with fisheries in New England before moving to Alaska in 1987. She is currently a professor and marine mammal specialist for the Alaska Sea Grant Marine Advisory Program, University of Alaska Fairbanks.

Because Wynne believes informed and enthusiastic resource users are vital to collecting reliable scientific data about marine resources, she wrote *Guide to Marine Mammals of Alaska* in 1993. The success and proven utility of that book inspired her to produce this companion guide for U.S. Atlantic waters, where identification of marine mammals and turtles is also problematic.

Kate Wynne/ASG

Malia Schwartz/RISG

Malia Schwartz

Malia Schwartz has been studying the diving physiology of marine and freshwater turtles since 1989. Her interest is driven by the persistent problems of marine turtle injury and death caused by accidental entanglement. With support from the Rhode Island Sea Grant Marine Extension Fisheries Program, she designed a recovery protocol for marine turtles found entangled in fishing gear. She has a master's degree in zoology and a Ph.D. in biological sciences from the University of Rhode Island.

In addition to her research, Schwartz served as communications director for Rhode Island Sea Grant, where she was responsible for translating the results of research and outreach programs into products that are understandable and useful for the public and decision-makers. This guide is an important part of that effort. Her hope is that those who use this guide will learn something new about these fascinating animals that inhabit our Atlantic waters.

Production of this guide was truly collaborative, joining a multiregional Sea Grant outreach effort with broad and enthusiastic support of local, state, and federal marine resource experts. Such collaboration attests to the recognized need and mutual desire to improve our understanding and conservation of marine mammal and turtle resources in U.S. Atlantic waters.

Funding was provided by the National Marine Fisheries Service (NMFS) Office of Protected Resources, Silver Spring, Md., and NMFS Northeast Region, Gloucester, Mass., and by the Alaska and Rhode Island Sea Grant College programs.

Species accounts were reviewed by Tim Cole, James Gilbert, Steve Katona, Robert Kenney, David Lavigne, James Mead, Keith Mullin, John Nicolas, Dan Odell, Mike Payne, Andy Read, Valerie Rough, Barbara Schroeder, Robert Shoop, Gordon Waring, and Randall Wells. We thank photographers from the Center for Coastal Studies (CCS), New England Aquarium (NEA), Mystic Aquarium (MA), National Aquarium in Baltimore (NAB), Marinelife Center of Juno Beach (MCJB), NMFS National Marine Mammal Laboratory (NMML), Texas A&M University (TAMU), URI Cetacean & Turtle Assessment Program (CETAP), University of Aberdeen, U.K. (UAUK), National Museum of Natural History, Smithsonian Institution (NMNH-SI), Memorial University of Newfoundland (MUN), and NMFS regional fisheries science centers—Southeast (Pascagoula, Miss.) (SEFSC), Northeast (Woods Hole, Mass.) (NEFSC), Alaska (Seattle, Wash.) (AFSC)—and others for graciously donating photos for our use.

Special thanks to Robert Kenney and Keith Mullin for their many comments and patient assistance, to Robert Kenney and Amy Williams for reviewing the final draft of this guide, and to Joseph DeAlteris and Sue Keller for bringing together talents at the Alaska and Rhode Island Sea Grant programs and financial resources to produce this guide.

Stuart Cromarty

ACKNOWLEDGMENTS

TABLE OF CONTENTS

Keith Mullin/SEFSC

Kate Wynne/ASG

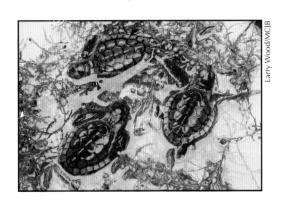

Larry Wood/MCJB

TABLE OF CONTENTS

Marine mammals and turtles have adapted to life in a three-dimensional environment to which humans are only brief and superficial visitors. For the most part, their lives remain a captivating mystery to us, punctuated by our brief encounters with those that surface within sight at sea or come ashore to rest, nest, breed, or die. Our knowledge of many marine mammal and turtle species is frustratingly limited, hampered by infrequent viewing opportunities and difficulties identifying those seen.

For the interested public, the ability to identify individual species is often the first step to appreciating the lives and conservation needs of marine mammals and turtles. But species identification is also key to improving our knowledge about these species, their distribution, their natural history, and the causes and impact of their deaths. Increasingly, accurate species identification is expected of fishermen, stranding network volunteers, and fishery

observers nationwide whose species-specific sightings, mortality, and bycatch data are used to manage the species and their interactions with humans.

This guide is designed to familiarize its users with distinguishing traits of the cetaceans, pinnipeds, manatee, and sea turtles commonly found in U.S. Atlantic waters, including the Gulf of Mexico, (see map on inside back cover) with references to U.S. Caribbean waters. Also included are less common species whose perceived "rarity" may be more a function of misidentification than actual scarcity. This guide's format is intended to encourage fast, accurate species identification using key physical and behavioral characteristics, distribution maps, and comparative surface profiles. It is designed to weather many seasons of sea duty by mariners, fishermen, and biologists. We hope it is equally informative for shore-based users of all ages and backgrounds.

Kate Wynne/ASG

Accurate identification of marine species at sea often requires rapid incorporation of many clues during brief and distant visual contact. The physical traits, location (geographic and local habitat), and behavior of the animal are all important clues to note when viewing marine mammals and turtles and differentiating among similar species.

Tips:

1. Know what characteristics to look for. Review guides prior to your trip and know what features are most helpful in species identification.

2. Be patient and persistent. Continue scanning the area—it may be several minutes before a marine mammal or turtle resurfaces.

3. Keep your eye on the animal: Make mental notes or brief sketches of key traits for later comparison with guides.

4. Don't jump to conclusions or base identification on behavior alone. Some marine mammal and turtle behavior is misleading (seals may porpoise, whales may sleep log-like at the surface, sea turtles occasionally breach). Use at least two physical characteristics to make a positive identification.

5. This guide is wire-bound, water-resistant, and specifically designed to aid fast and accurate identification at sea.

- Three color-coded sections separate cetaceans, seals/manatee, and sea turtles. Cetacean page margins are further marked to quickly distinguish smaller (less than 3 m) from larger species.

- Each section contains composite scale drawings, morphology and gender identification, and family characteristics.

- Concise individual species accounts are grouped by family and generally presented in descending order by adult size.

- Key species traits are presented in **bold** text.

- Silhouette surface profiles accentuate traits visible at sea under poor lighting.

- Detailed surface, head, or shell profiles are presented for easy comparison of species with similar traits and distribution.

- Range maps show *approximate* seasonal distribution of each species.
  Colors: pink = summer, blue = winter, purple = year-round, yellow line = known nesting grounds (turtles).
  Patterns: solid = known range, lines = assumed range or range extensions, arrows = migration routes, question marks = unknown seasonal location.

- Inside back cover shows entire area referenced in this guide.

- A glossary of terms and abbreviations used in the text and a list of further reading begin on page 110.

- Use of marine mammal names follows Rice (1998). See reference on page 112.

USING THIS GUIDE

Because they are mammals, cetaceans, pinnipeds, and manatees are endothermic (warm-blooded), have hair (at some time during life), and give birth to live young, which are suckled. Sea turtles are reptiles: They are ectothermic (cold-blooded), have scaly skin, and, like many reptiles, lay eggs. Although taxonomically distant, both groups breathe air through lungs and have evolved similar traits to allow them to survive successfully while being primarily submerged in a saltwater environment.

Marine Adaptations

Swimming Adaptations

- Streamlined body forms reduce drag through water.

- Powerful appendages allow for maximal propulsion and minimal drag to improve swimming efficiency.

Deep Diving

Generally, marine mammal and turtle lungs are proportionately smaller than humans' but they:

- Use oxygen very efficiently: They fill their lungs and can exchange 80–90% of their air in each breath. Their blood chemistry allows greater oxygen retention: During long dives, they can use oxygen chemically stored in their blood and muscles.

- Have a high tolerance to lactic acid and carbon dioxide. Their muscles can work anaerobically (without oxygen) while they hold their breath.

- Can tolerate tremendous atmospheric pressure at great depths. Lungs are collapsible, air spaces are minimized, and nitrogen absorption is limited, preventing the "bends."

Thermoregulation

- A large body with small surface-to-volume ratio reduces heat loss. Blubber or thick underfur is used as insulation.

- Complex circulatory system in the extremities is used to conserve and dissipate heat.

- Able to behaviorally regulate body temperature. Some sea turtles bask in the sun or swim vigorously, which elevates their metabolism, allowing them to remain warmer in cold water.

Water Conservation

Marine mammals and turtles are faced with the problem of conserving freshwater in a salty environment. As such, both groups:

- Utilize freshwater present in their food, inspired air, and blubber.

- Can remove excess salt from their bodies with specialized organs (kidneys in marine mammals, salt glands located above the eyes in sea turtles).

Sensory Adaptations

- Marine mammals communicate underwater with sound, and many species use sound (echolocation) to locate prey. Tactile senses are acute: Pinnipeds and manatees have well-developed facial whiskers.

- Sea turtles have poor hearing but good eyesight underwater.

Conservation Issues

In addition to sharing physiological challenges associated with their marine existence, marine mammals and turtles also share many human-related challenges. Entanglement in active and discarded fishing gear poses a serious threat to marine turtles and mammals, which must regularly reach the surface to breathe. Fishing methods, gear modifications (TEDs and pingers), and disentanglement techniques continue to be developed to reduce the likelihood of capture and to increase the survival of animals released from fishing gear. Resource managers may also restrict fishing activities in areas or at times when the potential for entanglement of mammals or turtles is high.

Where their coastal ranges overlap with human activities, marine mammals and turtles may also suffer from disturbance, boat collisions, exposure to contaminants, and loss of feeding or nesting/pupping habitat. For instance, sea turtle egg and hatchling survival are threatened where nesting beaches are destroyed or disturbed by coastal development, erosion control, beach restructuring, or artificial lighting.

Plastic bags and other debris drifting at sea are potentially lethal when they entangle or are consumed by marine mammals and turtles that mistake them for prey. Increased boat traffic in coastal waters is a growing threat to the endangered Florida manatee and other near-coastal species.

A major impediment to conservation of marine mammals and turtles is the lack of knowledge. A better understanding of the natural history and habitat requirements of these animals is needed to assure their future conservation.

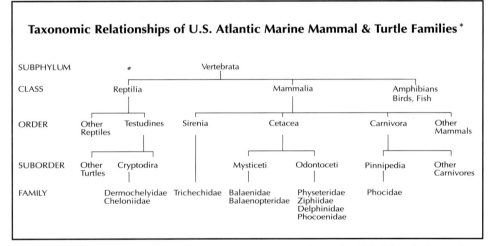

Taxonomic Relationships of U.S. Atlantic Marine Mammal & Turtle Families *

* **The taxonomic schemes used throughout this guide have been simplified for clarity, and are subject to change as our scientific understanding improves.**

Marine mammals and turtles are not randomly distributed in the oceans. Each species thrives in certain areas, or *habitats,* that support their specific energetic (food, thermoregulation) and reproductive needs.

Habitat

Food: The daily and seasonal distribution of marine predators is often dictated by the availability of their prey and is frequently associated with *edges* or areas of abrupt oceanographic change. Here, upwelling caused by changes in seafloor contour (or bathymetry) and currents and boundaries formed between discrete water masses promote plankton growth, concentration, and availability to marine consumers.

Reproduction: Adults of many species seasonally forgo the quest for food to accommodate special needs associated with producing and rearing offspring. Female turtles and seals leave their aquatic domain for protected, often traditional, land sites on which to nest or give birth. Many cetaceans migrate thousands of miles and fast for months in order to give birth

in warm waters needed by their cold-sensitive newborn calves. These nesting, pupping, and calving habitats often double as important breeding habitat, where adult males find large aggregations of receptive females with which to mate.

Figure 1. Advanced Very High Resolution Radiometer (AVHRR) image taken from the NOAA-11 satellite over Georges Bank. *Courtesy of NOAA Remote Sensing Group, NEFSC, Narragansett, R.I.*

Colors represent relaive water temperature, (red is warmest and blue is coolest).

Symbols show location of Risso's dolphin (+) and pilot whales (□) sighted during a July 1991 NMFS survey.

continental shelf edge (200 m)

Georges Bank

warm-core ring

Gulf Stream

north wall of Gulf Stream

Continental Shelf and Gulf Stream

The distribution of marine mammals and turtles in the Atlantic is greatly influenced by two oceanographic features, the continental shelf and the Gulf Stream (Fig. 1).

Continental Shelf: The North American continent forms a *shelf* that extends varying distances from shore until it reaches a depth of approximately 200 m. There, at the continental shelf *edge,* or break, the seafloor descends down a *slope* with varying steepness to great ocean depths (Fig. 2). The distribution of many marine mammals and turtles closely follows specific features of the shelf that support their prey. For instance, pilot whales and Risso's dolphin (and other squid-eating species) inhabit waters near the shelf edge (see Fig. 1) where the abundance of their primary prey is supported in part by areas of great mixing and upwelling.

Gulf Stream: The Gulf Stream is a strong ocean current that carries warm tropical waters into the Gulf of Mexico and north along the U.S. Atlantic coast until it veers eastward off the

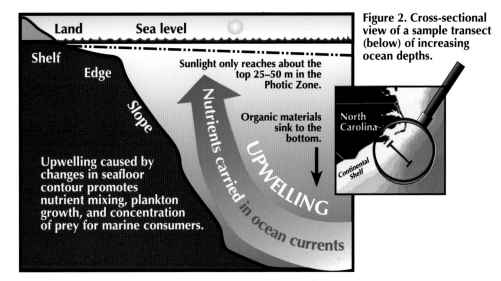

Figure 2. Cross-sectional view of a sample transect (below) of increasing ocean depths.

Land   Sea level

Shelf

Edge

Slope

Sunlight only reaches about the top 25–50 m in the Photic Zone.

Organic materials sink to the bottom.

Nutrients carried in ocean currents

UPWELLING

Upwelling caused by changes in seafloor contour promotes nutrient mixing, plankton growth, and concentration of prey for marine consumers.

North Carolina

Continental Shelf

mid-Atlantic. The warm, nutrient-poor Gulf Stream waters do not readily mix with the colder, productive polar waters they meet, so a distinct temperature edge is maintained between Gulf Stream and adjacent waters. As a result, the Gulf Stream forms a tongue of tropical water that extends north and provides habitat for warm-water species in otherwise

cold latitudes. On a smaller scale, the Gulf Stream generates warm-core rings and cold-core rings. These temperature anomalies may remain intact for several months, enhancing local productivity, concentrating prey, and thus providing important habitat features for many species (Fig. 1).

WHY ARE THEY WHERE THEY ARE?

Cetaceans are completely aquatic mammals: They feed, mate, calve, and suckle their young in the water. Because their bodies are constantly supported by water, animals in this order include some of Earth's largest species. Cetaceans are specialized swimmers: Some can sustain speeds up to 25 mph, may dive to 3,000 m (10,000 ft), or remain submerged up to two hours. Their bodies are smooth, streamlined, and hairless to reduce drag while swimming. Limbs are tapered or lacking and the tail is developed into horizontal flukes used for propulsion. All cetaceans have a subcutaneous layer of blubber that insulates them from cold water and acts as a fat reserve.

Cetaceans breathe through a single or divided blowhole on top of the head. As they surface after a dive, they forcefully exhale a moist lungful of air (blow) and inhale new air. The characteristics of the blow can aid in identification.

Cetaceans are grouped into two taxonomic suborders: the baleen whales (Mysticeti) and the toothed whales (Odontoceti). Mysticetes are filter feeders that catch zooplankton or small schooling fish by skimming or gulping large volumes of prey and water. The tongue then forces the water back out the mouth past hundreds of baleen plates that act as a sieve to trap prey, which are then swallowed. Odontocetes have a variable number of identical conical or spade-shaped teeth that are used to strain or grasp prey, primarily fish and squid.

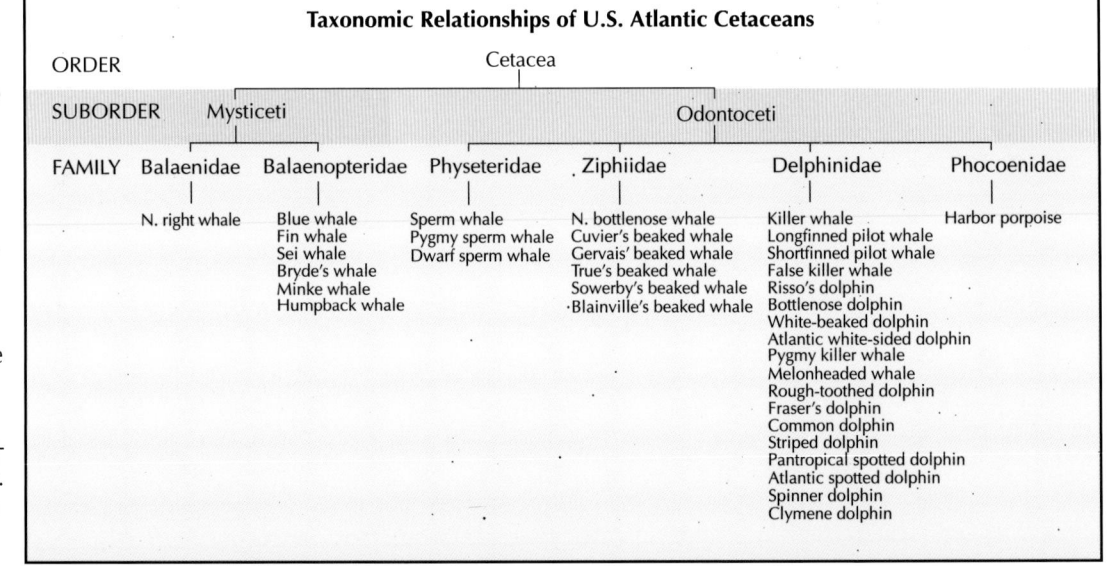

Taxonomic Relationships of U.S. Atlantic Cetaceans

ORDER	Cetacea					
SUBORDER	Mysticeti		Odontoceti			
FAMILY	Balaenidae	Balaenopteridae	Physeteridae	Ziphiidae	Delphinidae	Phocoenidae
	N. right whale	Blue whale Fin whale Sei whale Bryde's whale Minke whale Humpback whale	Sperm whale Pygmy sperm whale Dwarf sperm whale	N. bottlenose whale Cuvier's beaked whale Gervais' beaked whale True's beaked whale Sowerby's beaked whale Blainville's beaked whale	Killer whale Longfinned pilot whale Shortfinned pilot whale False killer whale Risso's dolphin Bottlenose dolphin White-beaked dolphin Atlantic white-sided dolphin Pygmy killer whale Melonheaded whale Rough-toothed dolphin Fraser's dolphin Common dolphin Striped dolphin Pantropical spotted dolphin Atlantic spotted dolphin Spinner dolphin Clymene dolphin	Harbor porpoise

Mysticeti (Baleen Whales)

All mysticetes have baleen and a divided blowhole. Females are generally larger than males but no other sexual dimorphism exists. They are not known to echolocate. Two of three extant families are represented in U.S. Atlantic waters.

Balaenidae
(Right Whales):
Rotund body
with massive

head and broad flukes. Narrow, arching rostrum (upper jaw) supports long baleen plates. No dorsal fin or ventral throat grooves are present. They skim-feed through large schools of zooplankton. Divergent blowhole creates a V-shaped blow.

Balaenopteridae
(Rorquals):
Slender body
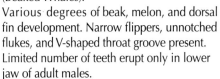
with dorsal fin. Numerous ventral throat grooves expand for gulping large volumes of water and prey. Single straight blow.

Odontoceti (Toothed Whales)

All odontocetes have a single blowhole. Sexual dimorphism is common—males are larger than females and diagnostic secondary sex traits are present in some families (differences in dorsal fins, tooth pattern). Tooth count is variable. Echolocation for prey is common.

Physeteridae
(Sperm Whales):
Squared head
with underslung
lower jaw. Blowhole located left of center. Functional teeth lacking in upper jaw.

Ziphiidae
(Beaked Whales):

Various degrees of beak, melon, and dorsal fin development. Narrow flippers, unnotched flukes, and V-shaped throat groove present. Limited number of teeth erupt only in lower jaw of adult males.

Delphinidae
(Dolphins and
"Blackfish"):
Beak present. Prominent dorsal fin, variable melon development. Conical teeth in both jaws (except Risso's dolphin).

Phocoenidae
(Porpoises):
Beak absent.

Triangular dorsal fin present. Spade-shaped teeth in both jaws.

MORPHOLOGY OF CETACEANS

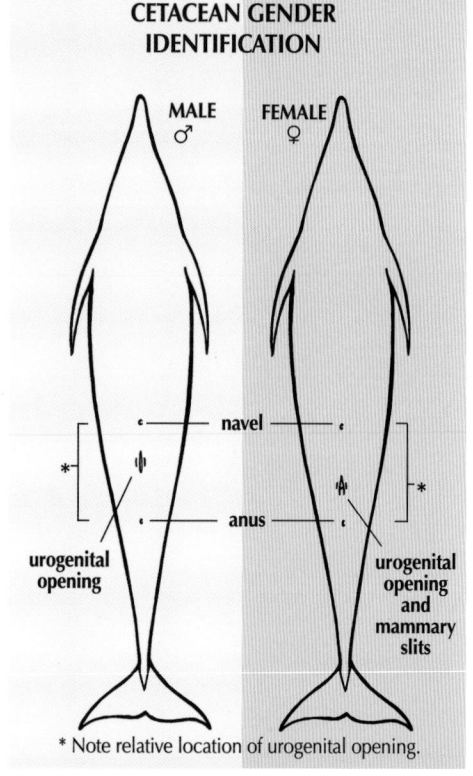

CETACEAN GENDER IDENTIFICATION

MALE ♂ FEMALE ♀

navel

anus

urogenital opening

urogenital opening and mammary slits

* Note relative location of urogenital opening.

MYSTICETE

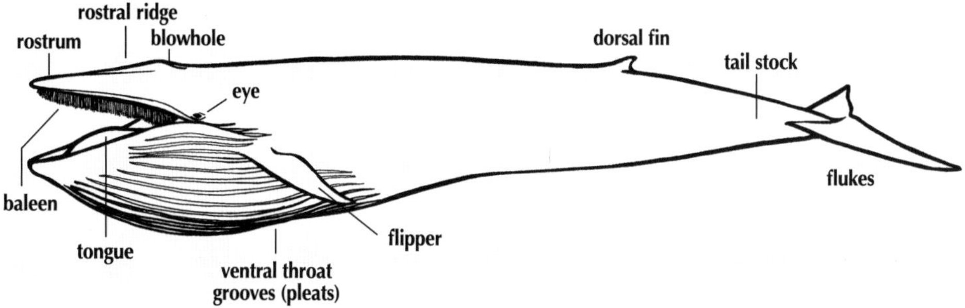

rostral ridge
rostrum
blowhole
eye
dorsal fin
tail stock
baleen
flukes
tongue
flipper
ventral throat grooves (pleats)

ODONTOCETE

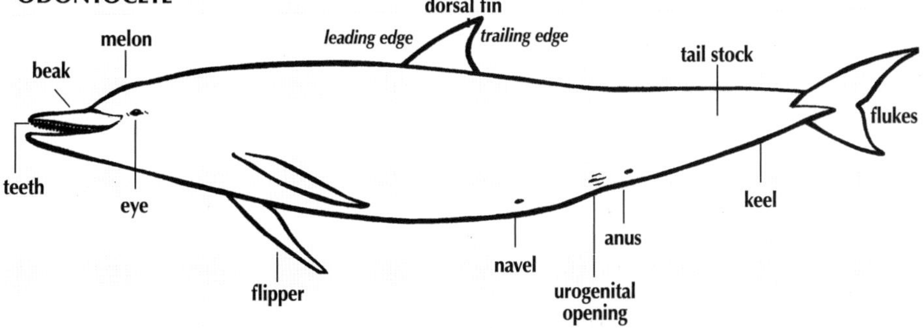

melon
beak
dorsal fin
leading edge *trailing edge*
tail stock
teeth
eye
flukes
flipper
navel
anus
urogenital opening
keel

BLUE WHALE

MINKE WHALE

FIN WHALE

SEI WHALE

BRYDE'S WHALE

HUMPBACK WHALE

NORTHERN RIGHT WHALE

6 FT

U.S. ATLANTIC CETACEANS: MYSTICETES

0	4.5 M
0	15 FT

9

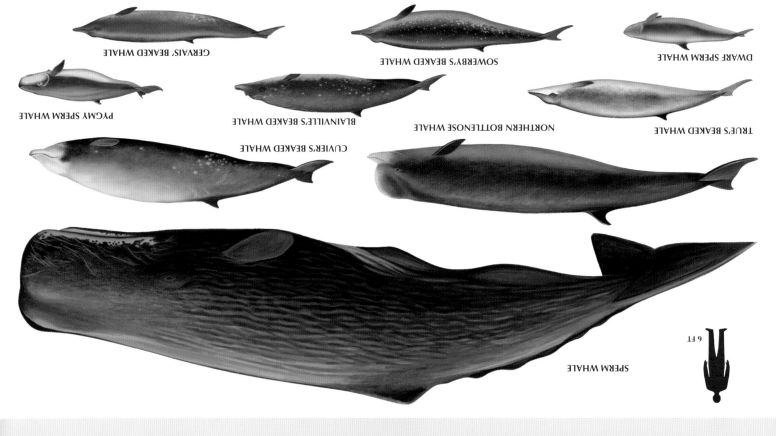

GERVAIS' BEAKED WHALE

SOWERBY'S BEAKED WHALE

DWARF SPERM WHALE

PYGMY SPERM WHALE

BLAINVILLE'S BEAKED WHALE

NORTHERN BOTTLENOSE WHALE

TRUE'S BEAKED WHALE

CUVIER'S BEAKED WHALE

SPERM WHALE

6 FT

U.S. ATLANTIC CETACEANS; ODONTOCETES

10

0   2.25 M
0   7.5 FT

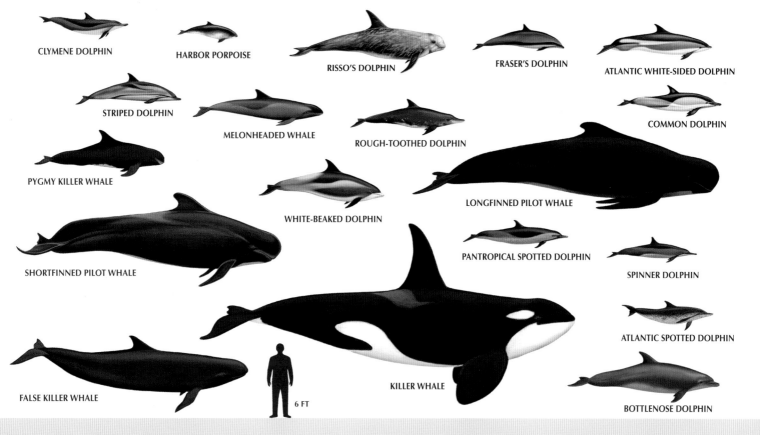

CLYMENE DOLPHIN

HARBOR PORPOISE

RISSO'S DOLPHIN

FRASER'S DOLPHIN

ATLANTIC WHITE-SIDED DOLPHIN

STRIPED DOLPHIN

MELONHEADED WHALE

ROUGH-TOOTHED DOLPHIN

COMMON DOLPHIN

PYGMY KILLER WHALE

WHITE-BEAKED DOLPHIN

LONGFINNED PILOT WHALE

PANTROPICAL SPOTTED DOLPHIN

SPINNER DOLPHIN

SHORTFINNED PILOT WHALE

ATLANTIC SPOTTED DOLPHIN

KILLER WHALE

FALSE KILLER WHALE

6 FT

BOTTLENOSE DOLPHIN

U.S. ATLANTIC CETACEANS: ODONTOCETES

0   2.25 M
0   7.5 FT

11

SIZE: Adults to 13-18 m (43-59 ft), 60 tons; females larger than males. At birth approx 4.5 m (15 ft).

BODY: Robust body with broad smooth back, large head (one-third body length); **narrow arching rostrum.** Wart-like **callosities** on rostrum, lower lip, and around eyes. Flippers broad and spatulate; large black flukes have smooth concave margin. **No throat grooves.**

COLOR: Predominantly black, often mottled, variable amount of white on belly.

BALEEN: Gray with fine bristles; 200-270 plates per side, to 2.2 m (7.2 ft) long.

DORSAL FIN: No dorsal fin.

BLOW: V-shaped, bushy to 5 m (16 ft) high.

BEHAVIOR: Docile, often approachable. Breaching, flipper slapping common. May be seen skim-feeding near surface with mouth agape. Groups of 2-3, but larger on feeding grounds.

DIVE PATTERN: Blow 5-10 times at 15-30 sec intervals then dive for 5-15 min. Usually show **flukes before deep dives.**

Northern Right Whale

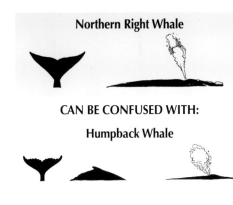

CAN BE CONFUSED WITH:

Humpback Whale

V-shaped blow, broad finless back, and narrow arching rostrum are characteristic of right whales.

Bob Bowman/CCS-Maine

DISTRIBUTION: N. Hemisphere. In w. N. Atlantic, summer Gulf of Maine to Newfoundland with concentration areas near MA and Nova Scotia. Wintering area(s) of most of population unknown, known calving areas off GA, FL.

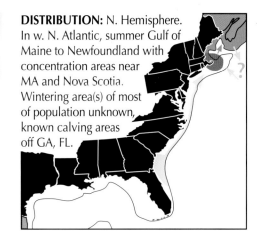

Baleen and callosities on rostrum are visible as right whale skim-feeds at surface.

Courtesy of CCS

HABITAT: Temperate waters. Critical feeding areas in Great South Channel, Cape Cod Bay, Bay of Fundy, and Scotian Shelf. Critical calving/rearing area in warm coastal waters off GA and FL.

DIET: Zooplankton, primarily copepods. Feed by skimming through dense concentrations of prey with mouth open.

LIFE HISTORY: Females sexually mature at 7–10 yrs. Thought to breed mostly in winter at low latitudes. Single calf every 3–4 yrs born fall-winter after gestation of ±12 mos. Lactation lasts 1 yr. May live 70 yrs.

STATUS AND HUMAN INTERACTIONS: Endangered, probably declining. Currently about 300 known in w. N. Atlantic waters. Harvested in U.S. Atlantic from 1650–1924, with a peak in early 1700s. Ship strikes and entanglement in fishing gear are current sources of human-caused mortality and may be hindering population growth and recovery.

NORTHERN RIGHT WHALE

Other names: North Atlantic right whale, *Eubalaena glacialis*

SIZE: Adults to 23–27 m (75–89 ft), 125 tons; females slightly larger than males. At birth approx 7 m (23 ft), 5,500 lbs. Record N. Atlantic length 28 m (92 ft). Earth's largest animal ever.

BODY: Long, sleek body. **Broad, flat, U-shaped rostrum** with prominent "splash guard" and single ridge forward of blowhole. Flippers long and slender; flukes nearly triangular with straight margin. Ventral throat grooves, 55–68, extend to navel.

COLOR: Body **blue-gray with light mottling.** Belly white, gray, or yellowish.

BALEEN: Black with dark coarse bristles; 270–400 broad plates per side, to 1 m (3 ft) long.

DORSAL FIN: Small, three-quarters back on body, to 0.3 m (1 ft) high. Often not seen until diving.

BLOW: Tall, dense (not bushy), vertical blow to 9 m (30 ft).

BEHAVIOR: Occur alone or in pairs. Fast swimmers (bursts of up to 20 mph). Dive to 150 m (490 ft) or more.

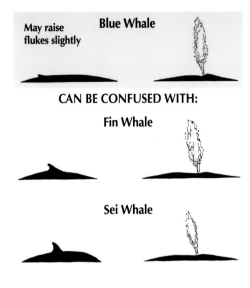

May raise flukes slightly

Blue Whale

CAN BE CONFUSED WITH:

Fin Whale

Sei Whale

DISTRIBUTION: Worldwide. In w. N. Atlantic, most frequently seen off e. Canada. Rare visitor in U.S. Atlantic. May range s. to FL and Gulf of Mexico in winter. Occasional summer sightings in New England waters.

The diminutive dorsal fin is located far back on the blue mottled body of a blue whale.

Rob Nawojchik/MA

DIVE PATTERN: Blow 8–15 times at 10–20 sec intervals, then dive for 3–20 min. **May briefly raise flukes parallel to water before deep dives.**

HABITAT: Generally pelagic. May concentrate in areas of dense krill concentrations on summer feeding grounds (e.g., Gulf of St. Lawrence).

DIET: Zooplankton, primarily krill (euphausiids). May consume an estimated 4 tons per day during peak summer feeding periods.

LIFE HISTORY: Sexually mature at 10 yrs. Breed and calve on winter range. Single calf every 2–3 yrs after gestation of 10–12 mos. Lactation lasts 7 mos. Calves gain ±91 kg (200 lbs) per day (3.6 kg per hr). May live 80 yrs.

STATUS AND HUMAN INTERACTIONS: Endangered. Estimated fewer than 1,500 in w. N. Atlantic; approx 300 individuals have been photo-catalogued in the Gulf of St. Lawrence. Estimated 350,000 were commercially harvested for their blubber (oil) from 1860s to 1960s, primarily in the S. Hemisphere.

BLUE WHALE

Other names: sulfur bottom

15

SIZE: Adults 17–24 m (56–79 ft), 70 tons. At birth approx 6.5 m (21 ft), 2 tons.

BODY: Long sleek body with flat, V-shaped rostrum. **Distinct ridge on back** from dorsal fin to **broad triangular flukes.** Ventral throat grooves, 55–100, extend to navel.

COLOR: Dark gray with light undersides, pale **chevron on back** behind head. Asymmetric jaw coloration: **lower right jaw white, lower left jaw dark.**

BALEEN: Right front plates white, others gray to white; 260–480 plates per side, to 0.7 m (27 in) long.

DORSAL FIN: Up to 0.6 m (2 ft) tall, falcate with blunt tip, two-thirds back on body. **Leading edge meets back smoothly at gentle angle.** Appears shortly after blow on shallow dives.

BLOW: Tall, elliptical, 5.5–6 m (18–20 ft) high.

BEHAVIOR: Occur singly or in groups of 2–10. May feed in large aggregations. Often associate with dolphins, other large whales. Fast swimmers (bursts to 20 mph); may breach.

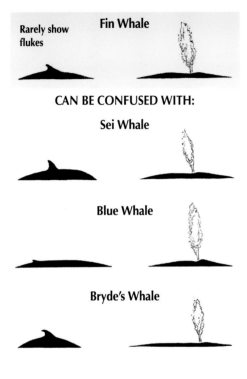

Rarely show flukes

Fin Whale

CAN BE CONFUSED WITH:

Sei Whale

Blue Whale

Bryde's Whale

DISTRIBUTION: Worldwide. In U.S. Atlantic, from Cape Hatteras north. Known major summer feeding grounds in New England. Winter calving and breeding grounds are unknown for most of population.

The white right jaw and prominent dorsal fin are visible as these fin whales surface (R) and dive (L). Note angle at which dorsal fin meets back.

Bob Bowman/CCS-Maine

DIVE PATTERN: Rarely show flukes. Blow 4–5 times at 10–20 sec intervals, then dive for 5–15 min. **Top of head and blow break surface together;** arch back and roll forward **exposing dorsal fin in wheel-like profile.**

HABITAT: Generally pelagic but also use deep coastal waters. Feed on continental shelf in waters to 200 m (650 ft) deep.

DIET: Variety of small schooling fish (herring, capelin, sand lance), squid, and planktonic crustaceans. Gulp large swarms, often while swimming on their right side.

LIFE HISTORY: Sexually mature at 6–12 yrs. Single calf every 2–3 yrs born Oct–Jan after gestation of 11–12 mos. Lactation lasts 6–7 mos. May live 90 yrs.

STATUS AND HUMAN INTERACTIONS: Endangered but common and probably increasing. Population estimated at 35,000 in N. Atlantic, with 2,700–6,000 in U.S. Atlantic waters. Commercial harvest ended in N. Atlantic in 1971.

FIN WHALE

SIZE: Adults to 18 m (59 ft); 30 tons; females slightly larger than males. At birth approx 4.5 m (15 ft).

BODY: Sleek dark body. Moderately pointed rostrum curves down to tip and sides. **Single rostral ridge** from blowhole to snout. Flippers slender and pointed. **Short ventral throat grooves**, 36–55, stop forward of navel.

COLOR: Dark gray to nearly black with pale belly. Frequent light mottling and patches. **Both lower lips gray.**

BALEEN: Dark gray with fine white bristles; 318–340 plates per side, to 0.8 m (31 in) long.

DORSAL FIN: Tall, erect, and strongly falcate. **Leading edge meets back at steep angle** two-thirds back on body.

BLOW: Elliptical, to 3 m (10 ft) high.

BEHAVIOR: Groups of 2–5. May associate with humpback and fin whales on feeding grounds. Fast swimmers that may change direction erratically.

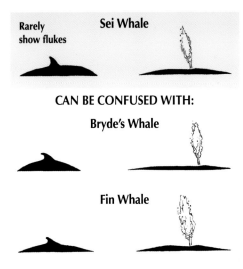

Rarely show flukes

Sei Whale

CAN BE CONFUSED WITH:

Bryde's Whale

Fin Whale

Sei whales have a single rostral ridge and fine white bristles on dark gray baleen.

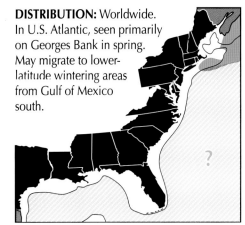

DISTRIBUTION: Worldwide. In U.S. Atlantic, seen primarily on Georges Bank in spring. May migrate to lower-latitude wintering areas from Gulf of Mexico south.

Tim Cole

DIVE PATTERN: Break surface with tip of rostrum. Back remains visible longer than for other large whales, then **dorsal fin sinks slowly straight down rather than wheeling forward like fin whale.** Blow 2–3 times between short dives (5–6 min); 5–6 times between long dives (15–30 min). **Seldom arch back or show flukes when diving.**

HABITAT: Generally pelagic but may follow prey inshore. Often found near shelf edge.

DIET: Primarily copepods and euphausiids. Skim through schools of crustaceans, often leaving trail of bubbles just prior to surfacing.

LIFE HISTORY: Sexually mature at 10 yrs. Breed in winter. Single calf every 2–3 yrs after gestation of 10–12 mos. Lactation lasts 7 mos. May live 70 yrs.

STATUS AND HUMAN INTERACTIONS: Endangered. Nova Scotian stock (includes those seen in Gulf of Maine) estimated at 1,400–2,200. Commercially harvested world-wide until 1986 for meat and oil. Harvest continued in Iceland into the 1990s.

SEI WHALE (pronounced "say" or "sigh")

Other names: pollock whale, sardine whale, coalfish whale

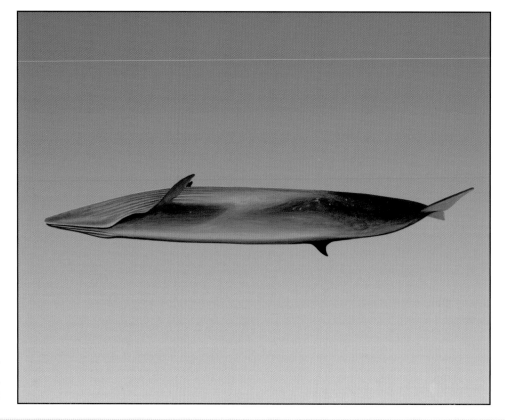

SIZE: Adults to 13–15.5 m (43–51 ft), 30 tons; females slightly larger than males. At birth approx 3.4 m (11 ft).

BODY: Slender dark body with moderately pointed, **slightly arched rostrum with three prominent ridges.** Flippers slender and pointed. **Long ventral throat grooves,** 40–70, extend past navel.

COLOR: Uniformly dark gray with pale to pink belly, some pale blotches. **Both lower lips uniformly gray.**

BALEEN: Dark gray with coarse gray bristles; 250–350 short plates per side, to 0.4 m (16 in) long.

DORSAL FIN: Tall, pointed, strongly falcate, less than two-thirds back on body. **Trailing edge often ragged.**

BLOW: Elliptical, to 3 m (10 ft) tall.

BEHAVIOR: May approach boats. Occur singly or in small groups but may form loose aggregations on feeding grounds.

Don't show flukes

Bryde's Whale

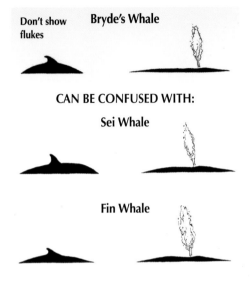

CAN BE CONFUSED WITH:

Sei Whale

Fin Whale

DISTRIBUTION: Worldwide, primarily between 40°N and 40°S latitudes. In U.S. Atlantic, range from Gulf of Mexico to Chesapeake Bay.

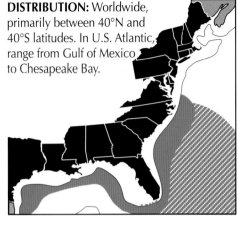

Bryde's whale—the only mysticete common in the Gulf of Mexico—has three ridges on its rostrum and both lower lips are dark.

Carrie Hubard/SEFSC

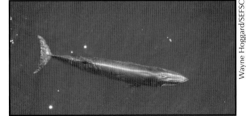

Wayne Hoggard/SEFSC

DIVE PATTERN: Often surface at steep angle, show much of head, **roll sharply and arch back. Do not show flukes** when diving. Irregular dive pattern and surface interval but avg 4–7 blows followed by dive of 2–8 min (max of 20 min).

HABITAT: Tropical, subtropical, or warm and productive temperate waters.

DIET: Variety of small schooling fish, squid, euphausiids. Often feed on their side, churning water and accelerating abruptly.

LIFE HISTORY: Sexually mature at 9–13 yrs. Peak breeding and calving in autumn. Single calf every 2 yrs after gestation of 10–12 mos. Lactation probably lasts <12 mos.

STATUS AND HUMAN INTERACTIONS: Status unknown. Estimated minimum of 218 in Gulf of Mexico, but **abundance and range may be underrepresented because of difficulty distinguishing from sei whales.**

BRYDE'S WHALE (pronounced "brood-uhs")

Other names: tropical whale, *B. edeni*

Balaenoptera acutorostrata
Family: Balaenopteridae

SIZE: Adults to 9–10 m (29–33 ft), 10 tons; females slightly larger than males. At birth approx. 2.8 m (9 ft).

BODY: Small, sleek body. **Head is sharply pointed** with flat rostrum. Flippers pointed, flukes broad. Ventral throat grooves, 50–70, extend to navel. Smallest baleen whale in N. Atlantic.

COLOR: Black or dark steel-gray. Lighter undersides, often with a pale chevron on back behind head. **White band on both flippers.**

BALEEN: Gray to white with fine white bristles; 230–325 plates per side, to 0.3 m (1 ft) long.

DORSAL FIN: Prominent and falcate, two-thirds back on body. **Appears simultaneously with blow.**

BLOW: Low, bushy, and inconspicuous.

BEHAVIOR: Fast swimmers, often approach boats. Solitary or in groups of 2–3. May breach; body leaves water at ±45° angle.

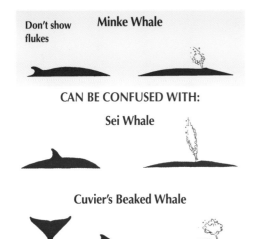

Minke Whale

Don't show flukes

CAN BE CONFUSED WITH:

Sei Whale

Cuvier's Beaked Whale

DISTRIBUTION: Worldwide. In U.S. Atlantic, range from Gulf of Mexico north. Greatest abundance in New England Apr–Nov. Likely winter offshore and in Caribbean.

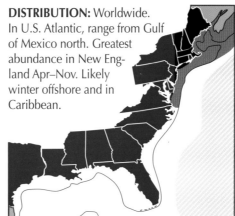

The dorsal fin is particularly prominent on a minke's small back.

Bob Bowman/CCS-Maine

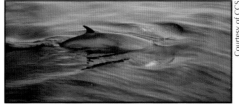

Courtesy of CCS

The pointed rostrum and white flipper patch are visible as this minke surfaces.

DIVE PATTERN: Rostrum breaks surface first. Blow 2–3 times at 30 sec intervals, then dive 3–20 min. Arch tail stock high but **don't show flukes.**

HABITAT: Pelagic, but also common in bays and shallow coastal waters. Widespread on shelf in summer, probably offshore in winter.

DIET: Variety of schooling fish (herring, capelin, sand lance, cod, mackerel), squid, and zooplankton (euphausiids and copepods).

LIFE HISTORY: Sexually mature at 6–8 yrs. Probably breed winter to early spring. Single calf every 1–2 yrs born Oct–Mar after gestation of 10–11 mos. Lactation lasts 3–6 mos. May live >50 yrs.

STATUS AND HUMAN INTERACTIONS: Common. No estimate for w. N. Atlantic, but up to 13,000 may use U.S. Atlantic waters. Are exposed to coastal hazards including entanglement in a variety of fixed fishing gear. Harvested in Newfoundland until 1972, primarily for meat and oil.

MINKE WHALE (pronounced "MINK-ee")

Other names: piked whale, little finner   23

HUMPBACK WHALE

SIZE: Adults to 11–16 m (36–52 ft), 40 tons; females slightly larger than males. At birth approx 5 m (16 ft), 2 tons.

BODY: Stout body with flat, broad head. Series of fleshy knobs on rostrum and lower lip. **Flippers long** (one-third body length) and **flukes long with irregular trailing edge.** Ventral throat grooves, 12–36, extend to navel.

COLOR: Black with white on throat and belly. **Variable amount of white on underside of flukes and both sides of flippers.**

BALEEN: Black with dark gray bristles; 270–400 plates per side, to 0.7 m (2 ft) long.

DORSAL FIN: Small with a broad base, raised hump in front, and "knuckles" behind. Shape varies. Seen at same time as blow.

BLOW: Broad and bushy, to 3 m (10 ft) high.

BEHAVIOR: Groups of 2–12, may form larger aggregations. **Acrobatic:** often breach, flipper slap, spyhop, and lobtail. Associate with minke, fin whale, and Atlantic white-sided dolphin.

Humpback Whale

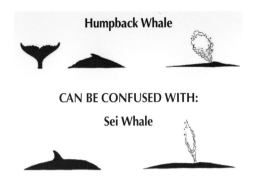

CAN BE CONFUSED WITH:

Sei Whale

Humpbacks have long flippers and a broad flat rostrum with sensory knobs.

DISTRIBUTION: Worldwide. In w. N. Atlantic, most winter in Caribbean and migrate to summer feeding grounds from Gulf of Maine to Iceland. Increased sightings off U.S. mid-Atlantic and s.e. states since mid-1980s.

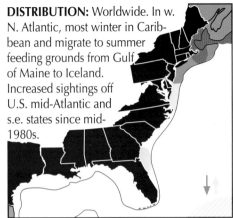

Distinctive markings on the underside of flukes are used to identify individual humpbacks.

Greg Stone/NEA

Bob Bowman/CCS-Maine

DIVE PATTERN: Blow 4–10 times at 20–30 sec intervals between dives lasting 3–7 min. Arch back, **show flukes prior to deep dives.**

HABITAT: Pelagic and coastal. Feed and breed over shallow banks, but may traverse open ocean during migration.

DIET: Small schooling fish (herring, sand lance, capelin) and krill. Lunge through and gulp concentrated prey, sometimes after generating a bubble net around the prey.

LIFE HISTORY: Sexually mature at 4–6 yrs. Single calf born every 2–3 yrs after gestation of 11–12 mos. Lactation lasts up to 1 yr. Breed and calve Jan–Mar in West Indies. May live 48 yrs.

STATUS AND HUMAN INTERACTIONS: Endangered. Approximately 8,000–10,000 in N. Atlantic, with approx 300–700 using U.S. Atlantic waters. Commercially overexploited from 1800s until protected from commercial harvest in 1966. Ship collisions and entanglement in fixed fishing gear may be significant sources of human-caused mortality.

HUMPBACK WHALE

SIZE: Adult males to 18 m (59 ft), 68 tons. Adult females to 12 m (39 ft), 18 tons. At birth approx 4 m (13 ft), 1 ton.

BODY: Huge, **squared head** (one-third body length) with **narrow underslung lower jaw. Body** (except for head) **appears wrinkled.** Large triangular flukes with smooth edges and deep notch.

COLOR: Dark gray-brown, some lighter blotches on belly and scarring around head.

TEETH: Large, conical; 36–50 **in lower jaw** only.

DORSAL FIN: Single, smooth, low dorsal hump followed by series of "knuckles."

BLOW: Off-center, single blowhole on front left corner of head. **Blow 4 m (13 ft) tall,** goes **forward at 45° angle and to left.**

BEHAVIOR: Females and young form "breeding schools" of 10–80 animals. Sexually inactive males form "bachelor schools"; oldest males are often solitary except for brief stays with breeding schools in mating season. Often encountered **resting log-like** at surface.

Sperm Whale

CAN BE CONFUSED WITH:

N. Bottlenose Whale

Blowhole location, wrinkles, and rounded dorsal fin are visible on these sperm whale females and calf.

Casey Hessinger/NEFSC

DISTRIBUTION: Worldwide, between 60°N and 60°S latitudes. In U.S. waters, present year-round in Gulf of Mexico and from NC to Georges Bank.

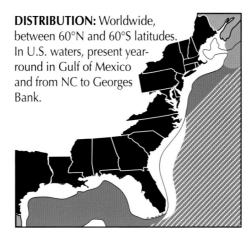

Group of sperm whales "logging" or resting with backs above surface.

Casey Hessinger/NEFSC

DIVE PATTERN: Deepest and longest diving cetacean known (dive up to 2 hrs, possibly to 3,000 m [9,800 ft]). Swim slowly at surface for 15–60 min blowing at regular intervals. **Usually show flukes when diving.**

HABITAT: Pelagic, usually deep waters near shelf edge, slope, and mid-ocean. Also on shelf in waters less than 200 m deep (650 ft) in spring and fall. Associated with Gulf Stream features.

DIET: Squid specialist, also fish. May eat 1 ton of squid per day.

LIFE HISTORY: Females sexually mature at 7–11 yrs; sexually mature males (>19 yrs) join female schools during mating season. Single calf born every 3–6 yrs in Jul–Nov after 14–16 mos gestation. Lactation lasts 12–24 mos.

STATUS AND HUMAN INTERACTIONS: Endangered but fairly common offshore. Minimum 2,700 from NC n., and 530 in Gulf of Mexico. Mass strandings fairly common. Incidentally caught in U.S. pelagic drift gillnets.

SPERM WHALE

Other names: cachalot, *P. catodon*   27

SIZE: Adults 3–3.7 m (10–12 ft), 400 kg. At birth approx 1.2 m (4 ft), 55 kg.

BODY: Short, **robust body** with squared or **conical shark-like head with tiny underslung lower jaw. Short flippers located far forward.** Body may appear wrinkled. **No throat creases.** Blowhole left of center.

COLOR: Dark gray back, lighter down sides to white belly. Pale crescent-shaped **"false gill"** on each side between eye and flipper.

TEETH: Long, sharp, curve inward; 24–36 **in lower jaw only.**

DORSAL FIN: Tiny but falcate, located aft of mid-back.

BLOW: Low and inconspicuous.

BEHAVIOR: Solitary or in small groups. May be approached and startled while **floating motionless at surface.** May appear "lumpy" like a knotted branch. When startled, often excrete an ink-like substance, darkening the surrounding water.

Pygmy Sperm Whale

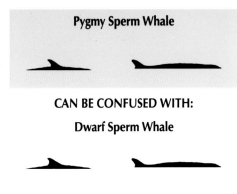

CAN BE CONFUSED WITH:

Dwarf Sperm Whale

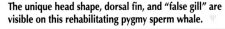

DISTRIBUTION: Worldwide in tropical to temperate oceanic waters. In U.S., sightings from Gulf of Mexico to mid-Atlantic with strandings as far n. as Nova Scotia.

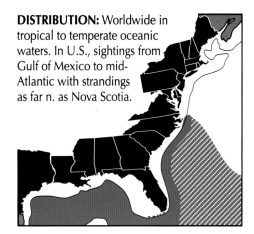

DIVE PATTERN: Deep, long diver. **After surfacing, sink inconspicuously without rolling. Seldom resighted.**

HABITAT: Pelagic; continental shelf edge, slope, and deep oceanic waters.

DIET: Squid, fish, and crustaceans.

LIFE HISTORY: Females sexually mature when 2.6–2.8 m long, males at 2.7–3.0 m. Single calf per yr born from fall to spring after 11 mos gestation. Lactation probably lasts 12 mos.

STATUS AND HUMAN INTERACTIONS: Abundance is uncertain but is second most common species stranding in the Southeast. Difficult to distinguish from dwarf sperm whale—combined *Kogia* spp. estimate of 420 in Atlantic (FL to Cape Hatteras) and approx 550 in Gulf of Mexico. Human-related mortality may result from consumption of plastic bags and ship strikes.

The unique head shape, dorsal fin, and "false gill" are visible on this rehabilitating pygmy sperm whale.

Courtesy of MA

Tim Cole

The number of long thin teeth in its tiny lower jaw help identify this stranded pygmy sperm whale.

PYGMY SPERM WHALE

<3 m (10 ft)

Other names: Kogia, lesser sperm whale, short-headed sperm whale

DWARF SPERM WHALE

SIZE: Adults 2.1–2.7 m (7–9 ft), 280 kg. At birth approx 1 m (3 ft), 45 kg.

BODY: Short, robust body. Small shark-like head with short slightly pointed snout and tiny underslung lower jaw. Short broad flippers **located far forward on body.** Several short throat creases. Body may appear wrinkled. Blowhole left of center.

COLOR: Dark gray back, lighter on sides to white belly. Pale crescent-shaped **"false gill"** behind each eye.

TEETH: Short, thin, curve inward; usually 16–22 **in lower jaw only;** may also have 2–6 smaller teeth in upper jaw.

DORSAL FIN: Dolphin-like, falcate, and erect. Located near mid-back.

BLOW: Low and inconspicuous.

BEHAVIOR: Solitary or in small groups. May be approached and startled **while floating motionless at surface** with head and back exposed. When startled, often excrete an ink-like substance, darkening the surrounding water. Commonly strand in the Southeast.

Dwarf Sperm Whale

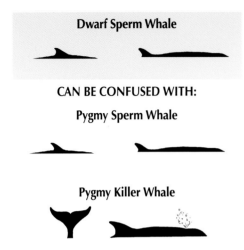

CAN BE CONFUSED WITH:

Pygmy Sperm Whale

Pygmy Killer Whale

When startled, both *Kogia* spp. may excrete an inky substance that forms a dark, presumably defensive, cloud behind them.

Rob Nawojchik/MA

DISTRIBUTION: Worldwide in tropical to temperate oceanic waters. In U.S., sightings from Gulf of Mexico to VA. Strandings as far n. as Nova Scotia.

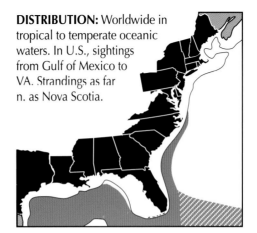

Wayne Hoggard/SEFSC

DIVE PATTERN: Deep, long divers. **Surface slowly and drop back under surface without rolling.**

HABITAT: Pelagic; generally use continental shelf edge, slope, and deep oceanic waters. May also use shelf waters.

DIET: Squid, fish, and crustaceans.

LIFE HISTORY: Sexually mature when 2.1–2.2 m long. Single calf born per yr from fall to spring after 9.5 mos gestation. Lactation probably lasts 12 mos.

STATUS AND HUMAN INTERACTIONS: Abundance uncertain; difficult to distinguish from pygmy sperm whale. Combined *Kogia* spp. minimum estimate of 420 in Atlantic (FL to Cape Hatteras) and 550 in Gulf of Mexico. Human-related mortality may result from consumption of plastic bags, ship strikes, and bycatch in pelagic fisheries.

Both *Kogia* spp. have a squared head and short flippers set far forward on their body visible even by air. They are most easily distinguished by dorsal fin shape.

DWARF SPERM WHALE

<3 m (10 ft)

Other names: Owen's pygmy sperm whale, *K. simus*

31

SIZE: Adult males to 9.8 m (32 ft), adult females to 8.7 m (29 ft). At birth approx 3.6 m (12 ft).

BODY: Robust body, wide back. **Bulbous head** with large melon and upturned dolphin-like beak. Short tapered flippers; **flukes broad and unnotched** with concave trailing edge.

COLOR: Body tan to gray with lighter scratches and scars. Head and neck white on large adults.

TEETH: One pair visible on adult males; conical, at tip of lower jaw.

DORSAL FIN: Darker than back. Prominent and falcate; located two-thirds back on body.

BLOW: Low, bushy, angled slightly forward; to 2 m (7 ft) high.

BEHAVIOR: Social; form tight pods of 5–15 animals, possibly segregated by sex.

DIVE PATTERN: Surface for 10+ min with regular breaths before diving for 1–2 hrs. **Often show head and beak when surfacing and flukes when diving.**

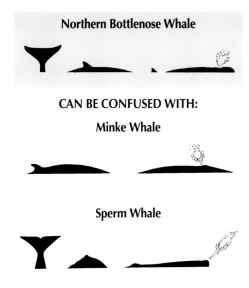

Northern Bottlenose Whale

CAN BE CONFUSED WITH:

Minke Whale

Sperm Whale

NOTE: All beaked whale sightings are significant: Photos and careful descriptions are needed!

DISTRIBUTION: N. Atlantic only; well-defined migration n. in summer and s. in winter. In U.S., rare sightings off n.e. coast with strandings as far s. as RI.

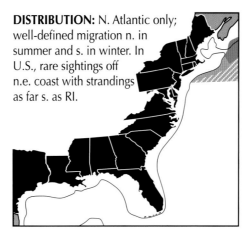

HABITAT: Pelagic in temperate to polar waters, often near ice edge. Prefer waters deeper than 1,000 m (3,280 ft). Many congregate in summer in "The Gully" off Nova Scotia.

DIET: Primarily squid, small deepwater fish.

LIFE HISTORY: Sexually mature at 7–11 yrs. Breed and calve in spring. Single calf every 2–3 yrs after 12 mos gestation. Lactation lasts 12+ mos. May live 37 yrs.

STATUS AND HUMAN INTERACTIONS: Uncommon in U.S. Atlantic. Commercially harvested in e. Canada until late 1960s for blubber and spermaceti (oil in head).

Elizabeth Moses/NEFSC

Note pale bulbous melon and dark dorsal fins of two northern bottlenose whales.

NORTHERN BOTTLENOSE WHALE

Other names: North Atlantic bottlenosed whale

33

SIZE: Adult males to 7 m (23 ft), adult females to 7.5 m (24.6 ft); 2–3 tons. At birth approx 2.7 m (8.8 ft).

BODY: Robust cigar-shaped body with small head. Sloping forehead and short beak with slightly curved gape. Short tapered flippers, flukes unnotched.

COLOR: Body mottled **golden tan to reddish brown.** Head and neck white in some adults. Scarring common. Dark eye patch.

TEETH: One pair visible on adult males; small, conical, at tip of lower jaw.

DORSAL FIN: Relatively small, falcate to triangular; located far aft.

BLOW: Low and inconspicuous.

BEHAVIOR: Travel in pods of 2–25. Apparently avoid vessels. May breach.

DIVE PATTERN: Several blows at 20 sec intervals before 20–40 min dives. **Forehead breaks surface but beak not usually visible.** Show flukes prior to deep dives.

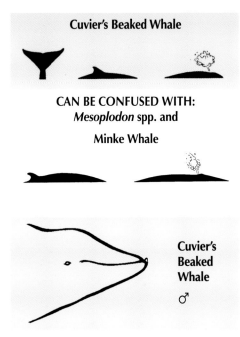

Cuvier's Beaked Whale

CAN BE CONFUSED WITH:
Mesoplodon spp. and

Minke Whale

Cuvier's
Beaked
Whale
♂

NOTE: All beaked whale sightings are significant: Photos and careful descriptions are needed!

DISTRIBUTION: Worldwide except polar waters. Strandings throughout U.S. Atlantic from Gulf of Mexico to Canada. Rare spring-summer sightings off n.e. U.S., year-round in Gulf of Mexico.

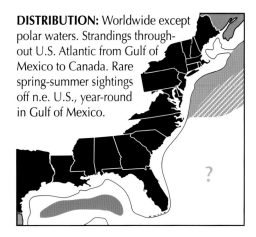

?

Cuvier's beaked whales have a single pair of small conical teeth at the tip of the lower jaw visible only on adult males.

Kate Wynne/ASG

HABITAT: Pelagic; shelf edge and waters deeper than 1,000 m (3,280 ft). Tropical to temperate waters; closely associated with Gulf Stream features.

DIET: Deepwater fish and squid.

LIFE HISTORY: Poorly known. Sexually mature at 7–11 yrs. Breed and calve in spring. Single calf every 2–3 yrs after 12 mos gestation. Lactation lasts 12+ mos. May live 35+ yrs.

STATUS AND HUMAN INTERACTIONS: Abundance and status uncertain due to difficulty distinguishing beaked whale species. Have been incidentally caught in pelagic Atlantic fisheries. **Most commonly stranded beaked whale in U.S. Atlantic.**

The unique head shape and color can often be seen as Cuvier's beaked whales surface.

Tim Cole

SIZE: Adult males to 4.6 m (15 ft), adult females to 5.2 m (17 ft). At birth approx 2.1 m (7 ft).

BODY: Slender body **laterally compressed** (taller than it is wide). **Small head has indentation at blowhole, prominent forehead, and slender beak. Short tapered flippers set low on body;** flukes unnotched.

COLOR: Dark gray back and sides. Belly lighter with irregular white blotches.

TEETH: One pair visible on adult males; small, triangular, located 10 cm (4 in) from tip of lower jaw.

DORSAL FIN: Small, falcate to triangular; located far aft.

BLOW: Low and inconspicuous.

BEHAVIOR: Little known. Few confirmed live Gervais' sightings.

DIVE PATTERN: Little known.

HABITAT: Pelagic; warm-temperate waters including Gulf Stream.

DIET: Squid and deepwater fish.

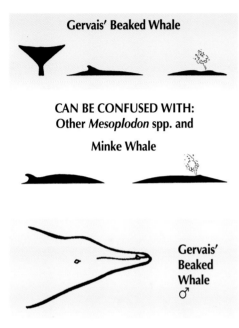

Gervais' Beaked Whale

CAN BE CONFUSED WITH:
Other *Mesoplodon* spp. and

Minke Whale

Gervais'
Beaked
Whale
♂

NOTE: All beaked whale sightings are significant: Photos and careful descriptions are needed!

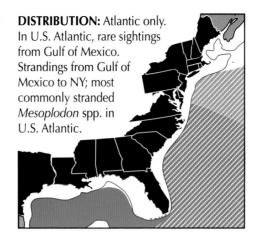

DISTRIBUTION: Atlantic only. In U.S. Atlantic, rare sightings from Gulf of Mexico. Strandings from Gulf of Mexico to NY; most commonly stranded *Mesoplodon* spp. in U.S. Atlantic.

Gervais' beaked whales have a small head with slightly sloping forehead.

James Mead/NMNH-SI

LIFE HISTORY: Poorly known. Females thought to be sexually mature at 4.5 m (15 ft). Known to live 27 yrs.

STATUS AND HUMAN INTERACTIONS: Abundance and status uncertain due to difficulty distinguishing beaked whale species. Have been incidentally caught in pelagic Atlantic fisheries.

Note location of the single pair of small triangular teeth visible on the lower jaw of this male Gervais' beaked whale.

Rob Nawojchik/MA

GERVAIS' BEAKED WHALE

Other names: Antillean beaked whale, Gulf Stream beaked whale

Mesopodon mirus
Family: Ziphiidae

SIZE: Adults to 5.3 m (17.4 ft), 1.4 tons. At birth approx 2.1 m (7 ft).

BODY: Robust, spindle-shaped body narrows toward tail. Small head with **dolphin-like beak and prominent melon delineated by slight indentation at blowhole. Sharp ridge** from dorsal fin to flukes. Short, tapered flippers; flukes unnotched.

COLOR: From few seen alive: **gray to brown back** with paler sides and belly. **Dark blaze along back** from melon past dorsal fin. Contrasting black dorsal fin, oval eye patch, and lips. Closely spaced parallel scarring on some animals.

TEETH: One pair visible on adult males; **small, conical teeth located at tip of straight lower jaw.**

DORSAL FIN: Darker than back. Small, falcate to triangular; located far aft.

BLOW: Low and inconspicuous.

BEHAVIOR: Little known.

True's Beaked Whale

CAN BE CONFUSED WITH:
Other *Mesoplodon* spp. and

Minke Whale

True's
Beaked
Whale
♂

NOTE: All beaked whale sightings are significant: Photos and careful descriptions are needed!

DISTRIBUTION: N. Atlantic only. In U.S. Atlantic, rare sightings and strandings n. of FL, particularly in the mid-Atlantic.

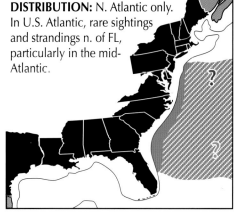

DIVE PATTERN: From few seen: several blows at 1–4 min intervals followed by longer dives. **Rostrum and eyes visible as whale surfaces.**

HABITAT: Pelagic; deep and temperate oceanic waters; may be associated with Gulf Stream.

DIET: Squid and deepwater fish.

LIFE HISTORY: Poorly known; no data.

STATUS AND HUMAN INTERACTIONS: Abundance and status uncertain due to difficulty distinguishing beaked whale species. Incidentally caught in pelagic Atlantic fisheries.

James Mead/NMNH-SI

One pair of conical teeth is visible at the tip of the lower jaw of this True's beaked whale.

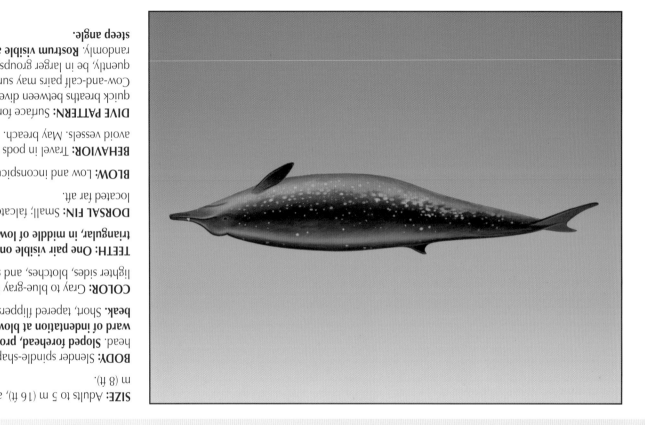

SIZE: Adults to 5 m (16 ft), at birth approx 2.4 m (8 ft).

BODY: Slender spindle-shaped body with small head. Sloped forehead, pronounced bulge forward of indentation at blowhole, long slender beak. Short, tapered flippers; flukes unnotched.

COLOR: Gray to blue-gray to brown back with lighter sides, blotches, and scratches.

TEETH: One pair visible on adult males; flat, triangular, in middle of lower jaw.

DORSAL FIN: Small; falcate to triangular; located far aft.

BLOW: Low and inconspicuous.

BEHAVIOR: Travel in pods of 2–25. Apparently avoid vessels. May breach.

DIVE PATTERN: Surface for 1 min taking 5–8 quick breaths between dives of 15–20 min. Cow-and-calf pairs may surface more frequently, be in larger groups, and swim more randomly. **Rostrum visible as whale surfaces at steep angle.**

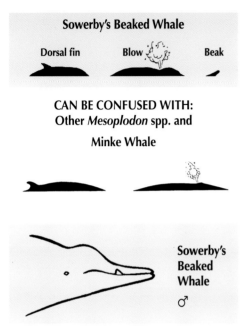

Sowerby's Beaked Whale

Dorsal fin	Blow	Beak

CAN BE CONFUSED WITH:
Other *Mesoplodon* spp. and

Minke Whale

Sowerby's Beaked Whale ♂

NOTE: All beaked whale sightings are significant: Photos and careful descriptions are needed!

DISTRIBUTION: N. Atlantic and Indian oceans only. In U.S. Atlantic, from New England north. Rare spring-summer sightings off Georges Bank. Strandings as far s. as FL.

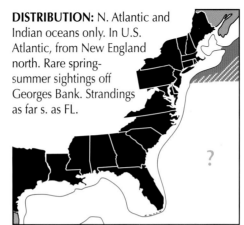

HABITAT: Pelagic; cold-temperate waters s. of pack ice.

DIET: Squid and deepwater fish.

LIFE HISTORY: Poorly known. Thought to breed and calve late winter/spring. Single calf born after 12 mos gestation. Lactation lasts 12+ mos.

STATUS AND HUMAN INTERACTIONS: Abundance uncertain due to difficulty distinguishing beaked whale species. Have been incidentally caught in pelagic Atlantic fisheries.

Scott F. Marion/NEA

The prominent beak and head shape are visible as Sowerby's beaked whales break surface at steep angle.

SOWERBY'S BEAKED WHALE

Other names: North Sea beaked whale

SIZE: Adults to 4.7 m (15 ft), 1 ton. At birth approx 2.1 m (7 ft).

BODY: Spindle-shaped body, thick moderate beak. **Forehead flattened** forward of blowhole. **High, prominent arch at corners of mouth.** Short, tapered flippers; flukes unnotched.

COLOR: Dark gray to black on back, lighter sides. Some have **large, pale oval blotches all over body.** Extensive scarring and scratches common.

TEETH: One pair visible on adult males; massive, flat, and triangular; tilt forward from top of mouthline arches (may have barnacles attached).

DORSAL FIN: Small; triangular to falcate; located far aft.

BLOW: Low and inconspicuous.

BEHAVIOR: Little known. Small groups, unobtrusive but may breach. Avoid vessels.

Blainville's Beaked Whale

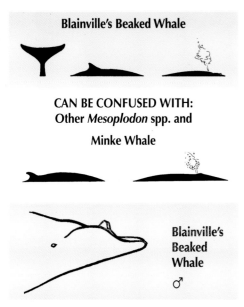

CAN BE CONFUSED WITH:
Other *Mesoplodon* spp. and
Minke Whale

Blainville's
Beaked
Whale
♂

NOTE: All beaked whale sightings are significant: Photos and careful descriptions are needed!

The arching lower jaw of Blainville's beaked whales is diagnostic even if teeth are not visible.

DISTRIBUTION: Worldwide in tropical to warm-temperate waters. In U.S. Atlantic, strandings have been reported from Gulf of Mexico to Canada.

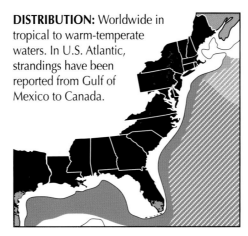

DIVE PATTERN: Several blows at 15–20 sec intervals before dives lasting 20–45 min or more. **Rostrum breaks surface at steep angle after deep dive.**

HABITAT: Pelagic. Deep, tropical to warm-temperate oceanic waters.

DIET: Fish and squid.

LIFE HISTORY: Poorly known. Thought to be sexually mature at 9–11 yrs.

STATUS AND HUMAN INTERACTIONS: Abundance and status uncertain due to difficulty distinguishing among beaked whale species. Have been incidentally caught in pelagic Atlantic fisheries.

James Mead/NMNH-SI

Rob Nawojchik/MA

KILLER WHALE

SIZE: Adult males to 9.5 m (31 ft), 8 tons. Adult females to 7 m (23 ft), 4 tons. At birth approx 2.4 m (8 ft), 180 kg.

BODY: Robust body. Round head with slight beak. Large paddle-like flippers.

COLOR: Striking contrast, black body with white chin, belly, and oval patch behind eye. Gray "saddle" behind dorsal fin.

TEETH: Large, conical; 20–26 upper row, 20–26 lower row.

DORSAL FIN: Prominent, mid-back. Sexually dimorphic: straight and tall on males (to 2 m [6 ft]); shorter and falcate on females.

BLOW: Bushy, to 3 m (10 ft) high.

BEHAVIOR: Highly social, often travel in pods of 3–55. Active at surface and acrobatic: breaching, spyhopping, and lobtailing are common. Fast swimmers (speeds to 25+ mph). Often cooperate in hunting and feeding efforts.

Killer Whale

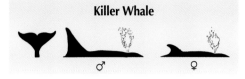

♂   ♀

CAN BE CONFUSED WITH:

Risso's Dolphin

False Killer Whale

Camille Goebel/NMML

DISTRIBUTION: Worldwide. In U.S. Atlantic, rare sightings from Gulf of Mexico but more common n. of NJ.

?

?

Stuart Cromarty

DIVE PATTERN: Variable. Many blows at short intervals between dives of 4–10 min.

HABITAT: Tropical to polar. Coastal waters to oceanic.

DIET: Most diverse cetacean diet; includes fish, birds, squid, turtles, and other marine mammals. In N. Pacific, diets of two recognized stocks differ: "Residents" eat primarily fish, while "transients" eat primarily marine mammals.

LIFE HISTORY: Sexually mature at 10–15 yrs. Mating may occur year-round. Single calf every 3–8 yrs after 17 mos gestation. Lactation lasts 12+ mos. May live >50 yrs.

STATUS AND HUMAN INTERACTIONS: Uncommon. An estimated 277 occur in the Gulf of Mexico but abundance and status off East Coast is unknown.

Like most delphinids, killer whales have conical teeth in both upper and lower jaws.

Far left: Killer whales have a prominent dorsal fin that is much taller and straighter on adult males than females.

KILLER WHALE

Other names: Orca   45

SIZE: Adult males to 7.6 m (25 ft), 2 tons. Adult females to 5.7 m (19 ft), 1.2 tons. At birth approx 1.7 m (5.5 ft), 80 kg.

BODY: Long robust body with thick tail stock (keel). **Bulbous head with prominent melon and slight beak. Sickle-shaped flippers are sharply pointed and long** (one-fifth of body length). Upturned mouthline.

COLOR: Black or dark gray except for light markings on throat, shoulder, and belly; may have faint saddle behind dorsal fin.

TEETH: Peg-like; 16–24 lower row, 16–24 upper row.

DORSAL FIN: Low but prominent, broad-based, falcate to flag-like; **located far forward on back.** May be rounded on adult males.

BLOW: Strong, to 1 m (3 ft) high.

BEHAVIOR: Gregarious, groups of 10s to 100s. Herds may rest together like logs at surface. Often associate with bottlenose and Atlantic white-sided dolphins.

Longfinned Pilot Whale

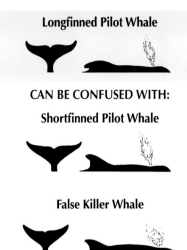

CAN BE CONFUSED WITH:

Shortfinned Pilot Whale

False Killer Whale

Low, broad-based dorsal fin is set far forward on the black body of longfinned pilot whales.

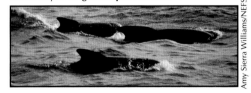

Amy Sierra Williams/NEFSC

DISTRIBUTION: All cold-temperate waters except N. Pacific. In w. N. Atlantic from Cape Hatteras n. to Greenland overlapping shortfinned pilot range in mid-Atlantic.

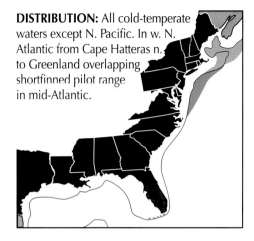

The melon, beak, and broad-based dorsal fin are visible on this group of longfinned pilot whales resting and spyhopping at surface.

Tim Cole

DIVE PATTERN: Several quick breaths followed by dives of 1–10 min. May show flukes when diving. Lobtailing, spyhopping, and mass strandings are common; **breaching and bow-riding are rare.**

HABITAT: "Anti-tropical," pelagic; continental shelf edge and slope, submerged banks, or associated with Gulf Stream north wall and thermal fronts. May move inshore in summer, offshore in winter following squid.

DIET: Primarily squid, also fish.

LIFE HISTORY: Sexually mature at 6–12 yrs. Breed Apr–Jun. Single calf every 3–3.5 yrs born Jun–Nov after 12–16 mos gestation. Lactation lasts 20+ mos. May live 50–70 yrs.

STATUS AND HUMAN INTERACTIONS: An estimated 8,200 occur from VA to Gulf of St. Lawrence. Have been incidentally caught in a variety of pelagic U.S. fisheries. May follow fishing vessels and forage from catch. Blubber samples show moderate levels of contaminants. A Newfoundland drive fishery for this species operated from 1947 to 1972.

LONGFINNED PILOT WHALE

Other names: blackfish, pothead, Atlantic or northern pilot whale, *G. melaena*

SHORTFINNED PILOT WHALE

SIZE: Adult males to 6 m (20 ft), 2 tons. Adult females to 5.2 m (17 ft), 1.2 tons. At birth approx 1.7 m (5.5 ft), 60 kg.

BODY: Long robust body with deep tail stock (keel). **Bulbous head** with prominent melon and slight beak. **Flippers gently curved, pointed, and less than one-sixth of body length.** Upturned mouthline.

COLOR: Brownish black or dark gray except for light markings on throat and belly; may have faint saddle behind dorsal fin.

TEETH: Peg-like; 14–18 upper row, 14–18 lower row.

DORSAL FIN: Low but prominent, broad-based; falcate to flag-like; **located far forward on back.** May be rounded on adult males.

BLOW: Strong, to 1 m (3 ft) high.

BEHAVIOR: Gregarious, groups of 10s to 100s. Herds may rest together like logs at surface. Lobtailing, spyhopping, and mass strandings are common; **breaching and bowriding are rare.** Often associate with bottlenose dolphins.

Shortfinned Pilot Whale

CAN BE CONFUSED WITH:

False Killer Whale

Longfinned Pilot Whale

Tim Cole

DISTRIBUTION: Worldwide in tropical and warm-temperate waters. In w. N. Atlantic from Gulf of Mexico to VA. Overlaps range of longfinned pilot in mid-Atlantic.

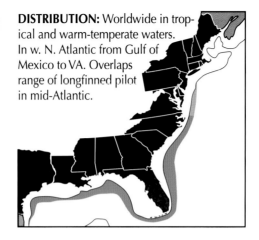

The bulbous head and dorsal fin location of pilot whales are visible from the air.

Wayne Hoggard/SEFSC

DIVE PATTERN: Several quick breaths followed by dives of 1–10 min. May show flukes when diving.

HABITAT: Tropical, pelagic to coastal; usually in Gulf Stream, along continental shelf and slope, or over submarine canyons. May move inshore in summer, offshore in winter to follow squid.

DIET: Primarily squid, also fish.

LIFE HISTORY: Speculated to be sexually mature at 6–12 yrs. Breed Apr–Jun. Single calf every 3–3.5 yrs born year-round after 15–16 mos gestation. Lactation lasts 20+ mos. May live 50–70 yrs.

STATUS AND HUMAN INTERACTIONS: Minimum population estimate of 350 in Gulf of Mexico and 750 from FL to Cape Hatteras. Have been incidentally caught in a variety of pelagic U.S. fisheries. Harvested in Caribbean into 1980s for oil and meat. Trained for oceanarium display.

A pale shoulder blaze is often visible on the brownish-black shortfinned pilot whale.

SHORTFINNED PILOT WHALE

Other names: blackfish, pothead, Pacific pilot whale

SIZE: Adult males to 5.5 m (18 ft), 1.4 tons. Adult females to 4.8 m (16 ft). At birth approx 1.8 m (6 ft), 175 lbs.

BODY: Slender body. **Small, narrow, tapered head** overhangs lower jaw; slight melon and no beak. **Distinctive hump on front margin of flippers.**

COLOR: All black except for faint patch on chest. **Black lips. No cape.**

TEETH: Large conical teeth; 16–22 upper row, 16–22 lower row.

DORSAL FIN: Tall, variably pointed, **strongly falcate; located mid-back.**

BLOW: Inconspicuous.

BEHAVIOR: Gregarious, groups of 10s to 100s. Often jump clear of water; may stop or change directions abruptly when feeding. Associate with bottlenose and other dolphins. **Only "blackfish" that frequently approaches boats and bowrides.** Mass strandings are common.

DIVE PATTERN: Whole head seen when surfacing.

False Killer Whale

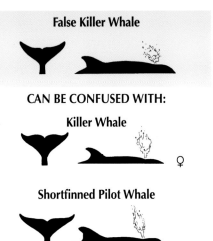

CAN BE CONFUSED WITH:

Killer Whale ♀

Shortfinned Pilot Whale

False killer whales have a narrow, tapered head and lack a dark cape on their back.

DISTRIBUTION: Worldwide in tropical and warm-temperate waters. In U.S. Atlantic waters, rare summer sightings from Gulf of Mexico to MD.

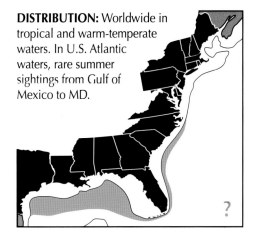

HABITAT: Pelagic; deep waters seaward of continental shelf.

DIET: Squid and fish. Known to attack other dolphins.

LIFE HISTORY: Sexually mature at 8–14 yrs. Mating and calving may occur year-round. Single calf every 3–4 yrs after 16 mos gestation. Lactation lasts 18 mos.

STATUS AND HUMAN INTERACTIONS: Uncommon in U.S. Atlantic. Minimum population estimate of 381 in n. Gulf of Mexico.

When visible, the curved leading edge of the flippers helps distinguish false killer whales from other "blackfish."

Carolyn Burks/SEFSC

Carrie Hubard/SEFSC

FALSE KILLER WHALE

Other names: blackfish

SIZE: Adults to 3–3.8 m (10–12.5 ft), 600 kg; males slightly larger than females. At birth approx 1.5 m (5 ft).

BODY: Robust torso with narrow tail stock. **Blunt head with squared melon but no beak.** Flippers long, dark, and pointed. Upturned mouthline. **Vertical crease in forehead.**

COLOR: Adults: light gray back and sides with darker dorsal fin, flippers, and flukes. White anchor patch on chest. Born light gray, darken to brown as subadults, then pale with age. Head and most of body white on older animals. **Extensive scarring common.**

TEETH: Thick and peg-like; fewer than 14, in **lower jaw only.**

DORSAL FIN: Very tall, slender, falcate, and variably pointed; located mid-back. **Darker than body.**

BEHAVIOR: Single to groups of 100s. May breach, spyhop, lobtail. Often found with other cetaceans, including pilot whales and bottle-nose dolphins. Generally avoid vessels and rarely bowride.

Risso's Dolphin

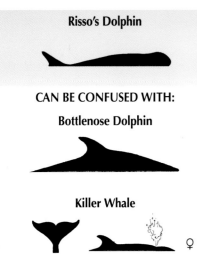

CAN BE CONFUSED WITH:

Bottlenose Dolphin

Killer Whale

♀

The squared beakless head and contrasting tall, dark dorsal fin on a light, scratched body distinguish Risso's from other dolphins.

DISTRIBUTION: Worldwide in tropical and warm-temperate waters. In U.S. Atlantic, n. Gulf of Mexico to mid-Atlantic year-round; range farther n. from spring to fall.

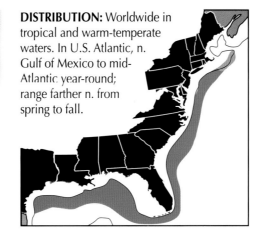

Keith Mullin/SEFSC

DIVE PATTERN: Take 10–12 breaths at 15–20 sec intervals prior to dives of 1–2 min. Max dive for 30 min. May show flukes when diving.

HABITAT: Pelagic; continental shelf edge and steep upper sections of slope (>100 m depths). Tropical and warm-temperate waters, Gulf Stream warm-core rings.

DIET: Squid specialist.

LIFE HISTORY: Little known. Thought to be sexually mature when 2.6–3 m in length. Max known age estimated at 17 years.

STATUS AND HUMAN INTERACTIONS: Fairly common. Estimated at 2,750 in n. Gulf of Mexico and 16,800 off East Coast. Have been incidentally caught in several U.S. Atlantic pelagic fisheries.

Note white head, dark dorsal fin, and scratches.

Amy Sierra Williams/NEFSC

RISSO'S DOLPHIN

<3 m (10 ft)

Other names: Grampus, gray grampus

SIZE: Adult size varies considerably: 1.9–3.6 m (6–12 ft), 140–650 kg. At birth approx 1 m (3 ft), 25 kg.

BODY: Robust body and head. **Short, thick, well-defined beak.** Two "ecotypes" are recognized: **"coastal form"** is shorter and slimmer than **larger "offshore form."** Flippers pointed, flukes deeply notched.

COLOR: Highly variable: blue-gray to brown with lighter sides and belly. **No distinctive color pattern.** Some have spots, pale shoulder blaze, or cape.

TEETH: Small, conical; 40–52 upper row, 36–48 lower row.

DORSAL FIN: Tall, falcate, with broad base; located mid-back.

BEHAVIOR: Coastal form: small groups <10; offshore form: groups of 10s to 100s. Acrobatic: breach, spyhop, lobtail. Often seen with pilot whales and right whales (in FL, GA).

DIVE PATTERN: Max dives of 3–4 min. **Beak rarely visible when surfacing.**

Bottlenose Dolphin

CAN BE CONFUSED WITH:

Risso's Dolphin

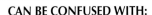

Atlantic Spotted Dolphin

Rough-toothed Dolphin

Bottlenose dolphins are robust with a short, thick beak and broad-based falcate dorsal fin. The coastal form (left) is shorter and slimmer than the offshore form (right).

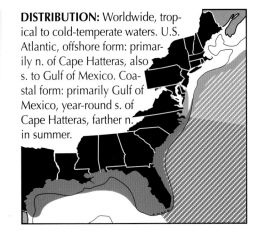

DISTRIBUTION: Worldwide, tropical to cold-temperate waters. U.S. Atlantic, offshore form: primarily n. of Cape Hatteras, also s. to Gulf of Mexico. Coastal form: primarily Gulf of Mexico, year-round s. of Cape Hatteras, farther n. in summer.

Randall Wells/MML

HABITAT: Coastal form: shallow, warm, inshore waters of bays and rivers. Offshore form: deep, offshore waters of shelf edge and slope.

DIET: Coastal form: variety of fish and invertebrates. Offshore form: squid, small fish.

LIFE HISTORY: Females sexually mature at 5–10 yrs, males at 8–12 yrs. Breed in spring and fall. Single calf every 3–6 yrs after gestation of 12 mos. Lactation lasts 12–18 mos. May live 50+ yrs.

STATUS AND HUMAN INTERACTIONS: Generally common but some coastal stocks are depleted. Estimated minimum of 19,070 in offshore stocks and 102,760 in coastal stocks. Both forms are killed accidentally in boat collisions and a variety of commercial and recreational fisheries. Common oceanarium performer.

Amy Sierra Williams/NEFSC

BOTTLENOSE DOLPHIN

<3 m (10 ft)

Other names: Atlantic bottlenosed dolphin, Tursiops

55

SIZE: Adults 3–3.2 m (10–10.5 ft), 275 kg. At birth approx 1.2 m (4 ft), 41 kg.

BODY: Robust body with thick tail stock (keel) and short, thick, pale beak. Moderately pointed flippers.

COLOR: Mostly black on back and sides, white from beak to belly. **White patch on side in front of dorsal fin and forming saddle behind dorsal fin.** Dorsal fin, flippers, and flukes black. **Beak white** to light brown.

TEETH: Sharp, conical; 44–56 upper row, 44–56 lower row.

DORSAL FIN: Tall, falcate, **with broad base;** located mid-back.

BEHAVIOR: Single to groups of 100s (in Canada). Fast swimmers; may breach, bowride. Have been seen with fin, killer, and other whales.

DIVE PATTERN: White beak and back visible when surfacing; may create rooster-tail spray.

HABITAT: Pelagic; cold-temperate to subarctic waters.

White-beaked Dolphin

CAN BE CONFUSED WITH:

Atlantic White-sided Dolphin

Common Dolphin

DISTRIBUTION: Northern N. Atlantic only, ranging n. to pack ice edge. In U.S. Atlantic, from New England north. Seen off Cape Cod and in Gulf of Maine Apr–Nov.

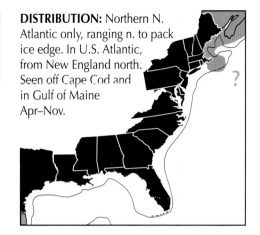

DIET: Squid, octopus, and variety of fish (including cod, herring, sand lance, haddock).

LIFE HISTORY: Little known. Sexually mature when 2.5 m (8 ft) in length. Breed in warm months. Single calf born Jun–Sep after gestation of ±12 mos.

STATUS AND HUMAN INTERACTIONS: Currently uncommon but no estimate for abundance in U.S. waters. Formerly common in Northeast but rarely seen there since 1970s, possibly in response to a change in prey availability.

Their white back distinguishes the white-beaked from other Atlantic dolphins.

Courtesy of MA

The white beak, saddle, and flanks are diagnostic on white-beaked dolphins.

Jon Lien/MUN

WHITE-BEAKED DOLPHIN

Other names: squid-hound

<3 m (10 ft)

SIZE: Adults 2.4–2.8 m (7.9–9.2 ft), 240 kg. At birth approx 1.2 m (4 ft), 32 kg.

BODY: Robust body with gently sloping forehead and thick keel. **Short, thick two-colored beak.** Flippers sickle-shaped and pointed.

COLOR: Black back, top of beak, flippers, and flukes. Gray sides, white belly. **White band below dorsal fin connects with yellow band on tail stock. Beak is black above and white below.**

TEETH: Sharp, conical; 58–80 upper row, 58–80 lower row.

DORSAL FIN: Tall, falcate, **sharply pointed with narrow base;** located mid-back.

BEHAVIOR: Small groups inshore, groups to 500+ offshore. Fast and acrobatic: breach, lobtail, infrequent bowrider. Associate with humpback, fin, and pilot whales. Strandings common.

DIVE PATTERN: Surface at 15–20 sec intervals. May leap clear of water or barely break surface.

Atlantic White-sided Dolphin

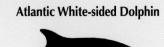

CAN BE CONFUSED WITH:

White-beaked Dolphin

Common Dolphin

DISTRIBUTION: Northern N. Atlantic only. In U.S. Atlantic, found n. of NC but concentrated in Gulf of Maine. May move inshore in summer and offshore in winter following prey.

HABITAT: Cold-temperate to subarctic waters over continental shelf and slope.

DIET: Variety of schooling fish and squid.

LIFE HISTORY: Sexually mature at 5–8 yrs. Breed May–Aug. Single calf every 2–3 yrs born Jun–Jul after gestation of 11 mos. Lactation lasts 12–18 mos. May live 27+ yrs.

STATUS AND HUMAN INTERACTIONS: Common. Approx 38,000–42,000 in U.S. Atlantic and possibly increasing. Have been incidentally caught in Atlantic trawls and gillnets. Moderate contaminant levels have been found in tissues.

The white side stripe and tan band behind the dorsal fin are visible as Atlantic white-sided dolphins surface.

Amy Sierra Williams/NEFSC

Female Atlantic white-sided dolphin and calf show their colors.

Bob Bowman/CCS-Maine

ATLANTIC WHITE-SIDED DOLPHIN

Other names: Lag, jumper

<3 m (10 ft)

SIZE: Adults 2.4–2.9 m (8–9.5 ft). At birth approx 0.8 m (32 in).

BODY: Slender body. Long, rounded head with slight melon and no beak. Flippers long with rounded tips.

COLOR: Dark body forms slender cape that dips slightly below dorsal fin; lighter sides. White lips, chin ("goatee"), and belly.

TEETH: Small, pointed; **16–22 upper row, 22–26 lower row.**

DORSAL FIN: Tall and falcate; located mid-back.

BEHAVIOR: Gregarious; groups of 15–50. Fast swimmers but may be seen "logging" on sunny days. Generally aggressive but often wary of boats.

DIVE PATTERN: Lively swimmer: **head comes completely out of water when surfacing, porpoise when swimming fast.** Large groups may swim abreast in coordinated line (**"chorus line"**) but bunch together when alarmed.

Pygmy Killer Whale

CAN BE CONFUSED WITH:

False Killer Whale

Melonheaded Whale

DISTRIBUTION: Worldwide in tropical and subtropical waters. In U.S. Atlantic waters, rare sightings from Gulf of Mexico n. to Cape Hatteras.

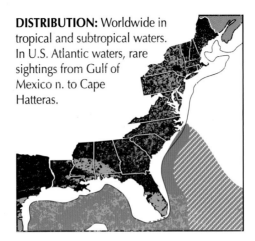

HABITAT: Pelagic; deep waters seaward of continental shelf.

DIET: Probably more fish than squid. Known to attack other dolphins.

LIFE HISTORY: Little known.

STATUS AND HUMAN INTERACTIONS: Status unknown; difficult to distinguish from melon-headed whale at sea. Minimum of 518 in n. Gulf of Mexico.

Pygmy killer whales have a narrow cape and long flippers with rounded tips.

A pygmy killer whale's rounded head is often seen when the whale surfaces.

PYGMY KILLER WHALE

Other names: slender blackfish

<3 m (10 ft)

61

MELONHEADED WHALE

SIZE: Adults 2.6–2.7 m (8.5–9 ft). At birth approx 0.8 m (32 in).

BODY: Long slim body with **slender tail stock.** Small head with somewhat pointed snout and no beak. Face narrows from eyes to snout—head looks beak-like or triangular from above. Flippers long, slender, and **sharply pointed.** Short, straight mouthline.

COLOR: Dark back and cape that dips far **down sides below dorsal fin;** lighter belly. Lips often white.

TEETH: Large number, small and pointed; 40–50 upper row, 40–50 lower row.

DORSAL FIN: Tall; falcate; located mid-back.

BEHAVIOR: Gregarious; groups to 1,500. Often associate with Fraser's, spinner, or pan-tropical spotted dolphins.

DIVE PATTERN: May form **tight herds** that surface or jump clear at **shallow angle with lots of spray** and make frequent course changes.

Melonheaded Whale

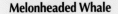

CAN BE CONFUSED WITH:

False Killer Whale

Pygmy Killer Whale

Melonheaded whales have a dark cape, sharply pointed flippers, and head that appears triangular from above.

DISTRIBUTION: Worldwide in tropical and subtropical waters. In U.S. Atlantic, sightings in Gulf of Mexico only; one stranding reported from MD.

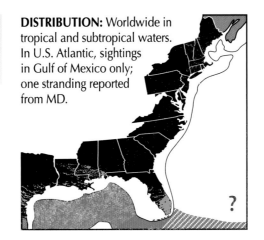

Keith Mullin/SEFSC

HABITAT: Pelagic; deep waters seaward of continental shelf.

DIET: Squid and variety of small fish. Known to attack small dolphins.

LIFE HISTORY: Little known. Thought to breed spring to summer and calve the following summer.

STATUS AND HUMAN INTERACTIONS: Status unknown. Population estimated at 4,000 in n. Gulf of Mexico.

Keith Mullin/SEFSC

Melonheaded whales form large, tight, fast-swimming herds, often with other dolphin species.

Keith Mullin/SEFSC

MELONHEADED WHALE

<3 m (10 ft)

Other names: many-toothed blackfish, Electra dolphin, little killer whale

63

SIZE: Adults 1.9–2.4 m (6–7.5 ft), 275 kg. At birth approx 1 m (3 ft).

BODY: Small, stocky body with narrow tail stock. Short beak is well defined. Small, thin, pointed flippers.

COLOR: Blue-gray back and sides, white belly. Most have a broad dark band from eye to anus beneath a smaller pale band that extends to tail stock. Flippers, dorsal fin, and flukes dark.

TEETH: Small, sharp, and conical; 40–80 upper row, 40–80 lower row.

DORSAL FIN: Small, triangular to falcate; located mid-back.

BEHAVIOR: Gregarious. Large groups of 10s to 1,000s. Associate with melonheaded whales and rough-toothed dolphins. Often shy and avoid ships.

DIVE PATTERN: Active swimmers that often **surface with spray.** Deep divers (250–500 m).

HABITAT: Pelagic, tropical. Avoid shallow, inshore waters.

Fraser's Dolphin

CAN BE CONFUSED WITH:

Striped Dolphin

Common Dolphin

Bottlenose Dolphin

DISTRIBUTION: Worldwide in temperate and tropical waters. In U.S. Atlantic, known only from deep waters of Gulf of Mexico.

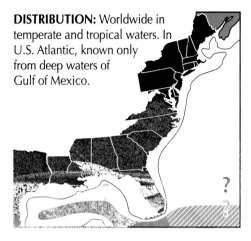

DIET: Squid, deepwater fish, shrimp.

LIFE HISTORY: Little known. Thought to be sexually mature at 7–8 yrs.

STATUS AND HUMAN INTERACTIONS: Uncommon. First seen alive in early 1970s. Estimated minimum of 127 in Gulf of Mexico.

Fraser's dolphins travel in large herds that generate lots of spray.

Scott Hill/NOAA Corps

Note the short beak, small triangular dorsal fin, and distinctive black band on side of this Fraser's dolphin.

Scott Hill/NOAA Corps

FRASER'S DOLPHIN

Other names: Sarawak dolphin

<3 m (10 ft)

COMMON DOLPHIN

Delphinus delphis (shortbeaked)
Delphinus capensis (longbeaked)
Family: Delphinidae

SIZE: Adults 2.3–2.6 m (7.5–8.5 ft), 135 kg. At birth approx 0.8 m (32 in).

BODY: Slender body with pale, slender tail stock. **Long pointed beak.** Flippers broad and slightly pointed.

COLOR: Distinctive black back and cape form **V-shaped saddle** that dips below dorsal fin. **Hourglass pattern on sides: tan patch (for-ward) and gray patch (aft)** cross below saddle. White chest and belly. **Black beak, eye ring, and line from jaw to flipper.**

TEETH: Small, sharp, and conical; 80–100 upper row, 80–100 lower row.

DORSAL FIN: Tall, falcate; located mid-back. **Usually dark with lighter center.**

BEHAVIOR: Gregarious; groups of 10s to 1,000s, often associate with other dolphins. Avid bowrider, seen riding fin in whale bow waves.

DIVE PATTERN: Fast and acrobatic: breach, porpoise, bowride. Max dives to 8 min.

Common Dolphin

CAN BE CONFUSED WITH:

Striped Dolphin

Clymene Dolphin

DISTRIBUTION: Worldwide, subtropical to temperate waters. In w. N. Atlantic, primarily n. of Cape Hatteras, rare sightings s. to FL. Common Jan–May from Cape Hatteras to Georges Bank; summer-fall on Georges Bank.

HABITAT: Pelagic; subtropical to temperate waters >100 fathoms. Longbeaked species more common inshore than shortbeaked species.

DIET: Variety of fish and squid.

LIFE HISTORY: Sexually mature at 3–5 yrs. Breed spring and fall. Single calf every yr after gestation of 10–11 mos. Lactation lasts 4 mos. May live 25–30 yrs.

STATUS AND HUMAN INTERACTIONS: Common but population trend unknown. Approx 22,000–45,000 from Cape Hatteras to Georges Bank. Incidentally killed in some Atlantic fisheries.

Note the long black beak, prominent dorsal fin, and distinctive coloration of this breaching common dolphin.

Scott Hill/NOAA Corps

Amy Sierra Williams/NEFSC

The distinctive V-shaped cape and hourglass color pattern are visible in these dorsal and lateral views of bowriding common dolphins.

COMMON DOLPHIN

<3 m (10 ft)

Other names: saddleback dolphin, criss-cross dolphin, hourglass dolphin

69

SIZE: Adults 2.2–2.6 m (7–8.5 ft), 130 kg. At birth approx 1 m (3 ft).

BODY: Slender body with narrow pale tail stock (no keel). Moderately long dark beak. Dark, slender, pointed flippers.

COLOR: Dark gray to brown cape (high near eye), bluish gray sides, and white to pink belly. Most have bold light blaze from shoulder toward dorsal fin, thick stripe ("bilge stripe") **from eye to anus. One or more dark bands** between eye and flipper.

TEETH: Small, sharp, and conical; 86–100 upper row, 86–100 lower row.

DORSAL FIN: Tall and thin, dark, falcate.

BEHAVIOR: Gregarious; groups of 100s to 1,000s, segregated by age and sex. Associate with common dolphins.

DIVE PATTERN: Max dives 5–10 min. Active swimmers—somersault and jump to 7 m (23 ft)—and may bowride.

Striped Dolphin

CAN BE CONFUSED WITH:

Atlantic Spotted Dolphin

Common Dolphin

Fraser's Dolphin

The diagnostic black "bilge stripe" and bold shoulder blaze are visible on these surfacing striped dolphins.

DISTRIBUTION: Worldwide in temperate to tropical oceans. In U.S. Atlantic, year-round from Cape Hatteras to Georges Bank; in Gulf of Mexico from fall to spring.

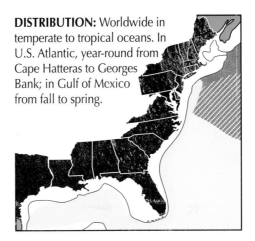

HABITAT: Pelagic; deep waters of continental shelf edge and slope. Associated with Gulf Stream n. wall and warm-core rings.

DIET: Deepwater squid, fish, shrimp.

LIFE HISTORY: Sexually mature at 5–9 yrs. Breed spring, fall, and winter. Single calf every 3 yrs after gestation of 12 mos. Lactation lasts 18 mos. May live 57+ yrs.

STATUS AND HUMAN INTERACTIONS: Estimated 31,700 from VA n.; minimum of 4,860 in n. Gulf of Mexico. Have been incidentally caught in some pelagic driftnet and trawl fisheries.

Scott Hill/NOAA Corps

Wayne Hoggard/SEFSC

STRIPED DOLPHIN

Other names: blue-white dolphin, white-belly, *S. styx*

<3 m (10 ft)

SIZE: Adults 1.6–2.6 m (5.2–8.5 ft), 120 kg. At birth approx 0.8 m (32 in).

BODY: Slender body with **long, narrow, white-tipped beak.** Keel pronounced in mature males. Flippers small, curved, and pointed.

COLOR: Bicolored background: dark back with light gray sides and belly. **Distinct cape is narrow at face, dips deeply forward of dorsal fin,** then narrows. **Small spots or flecks develop** with age and may cover adults. **White-tipped beak and lips. Dark band from beak to flipper;** may have dark ring around eye. **No shoulder blaze. Tail stock color is dark over light.**

TEETH: Small, sharp, and conical; 70–96 upper row, 68–94 lower row.

DORSAL FIN: Tall and slender, variably falcate; located mid-back.

BEHAVIOR: Gregarious; groups of few to 1,000s of mixed age and sex. Acrobatic, high-jumping bowriders.

DIVE PATTERN: Strong, fast, active swimmers: known speeds of 21.4 knots in 2.0 sec.

Pantropical Spotted Dolphin

CAN BE CONFUSED WITH:

Atlantic Spotted Dolphin

Spinner Dolphin

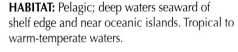

DISTRIBUTION: Worldwide in tropics and some warm-temperate waters. In w. N. Atlantic, year-round in n. Gulf of Mexico and offshore s.e. U.S. in winter.

HABITAT: Pelagic; deep waters seaward of shelf edge and near oceanic islands. Tropical to warm-temperate waters.

DIET: Squid and variety of schooling fish.

LIFE HISTORY: Sexually mature at 8–15 yrs. Breed spring and fall. Single calf every 1–5 yrs after gestation of 12 mos. Lactation lasts 3–5 yrs. May live 25–30 yrs.

STATUS AND HUMAN INTERACTIONS: Possibly most common offshore dolphin in the Southeast and Gulf of Mexico. Estimated minimum of 31,320 in Gulf of Mexico and 4,770 "undifferentiated spotted dolphins" (including both Atlantic and pantropical spotted dolphins) n. of VA. Have been incidentally caught in Atlantic pelagic driftnets and longlines.

Carol Roden/SEFSC

Wayne Hoggard/SEFSC

Note distinct cape, white beak tip, and dark-over-light tail stock of these "spotters."

PANTROPICAL SPOTTED DOLPHIN

<3 m (10 ft)

Other names: spotter, spotted dolphin, bridled dolphin

SIZE: Adults 2.1–2.3 m (7–7.5 ft), 140 kg. At birth approx 1 m (3 ft).

BODY: Fairly robust body with moderate keel. **Long, thick, white-tipped beak.** Flippers curved and pointed. Coastal animals larger and more spotted than offshore animals.

COLOR: Tricolored background: dark purplish gray back and cape, light gray sides, white belly. **Pale blaze** often sweeps up from side toward dorsal fin. **Variable spotting:** born unspotted, develop spots with age that may obliterate background color. **White-tipped beak. Tail stock single color,** pales with age.

TEETH: Small, sharp, and conical; 64–84 upper row, 60–80 lower row.

DORSAL FIN: Tall, dark, falcate; located mid-back.

BEHAVIOR: Gregarious; coastal groups of <20, offshore groups usually <100. Associate with other dolphins and small whales.

DIVE PATTERN: Tip of beak breaks surface first. Fast, acrobatic; avid bowrider.

Atlantic Spotted Dolphin

CAN BE CONFUSED WITH:

Bottlenose Dolphin

Rough-toothed Dolphin

DISTRIBUTION: Atlantic only. In w. N. Atlantic, s. New England to Gulf of Mexico.

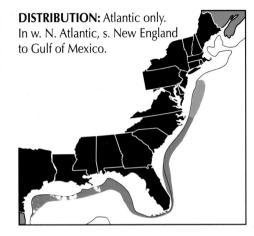

HABITAT: Coastal to pelagic. Tropical to warm-temperate waters over continental shelf, edge, and upper reaches of slope. Associated with Gulf Stream n. wall and warm core rings.

DIET: Squid and variety of fish.

LIFE HISTORY: Sexually mature at 8–15 yrs. Breed spring and fall. Single calf every 1–5 yrs after gestation of 12 mos. Lactation lasts 3–5 yrs. May live 25–30 yrs.

STATUS AND HUMAN INTERACTIONS: Estimated minimum of 3,200 in Gulf of Mexico and 4,770 "undifferentiated spotted dolphins" (including both Atlantic and pantropical spotted dolphins) on East Coast n. of VA. Have been incidentally caught in pelagic driftnets, longlines, and tuna purse seines.

Carol Roden/SEFSC

Amy Sierra Williams/NEFSC

Left: Atlantic spotted dolphins have a long white-tipped beak, variable spotting over a tricolored background, and a solid colored tail stock.

A light shoulder blaze is often visible on Atlantic spotted dolphins.

ATLANTIC SPOTTED DOLPHIN

<3 m (10 ft)

Other names: spotted dolphin, Frontalis, Gulf Stream spotted dolphin, *S. plagiodon*

SIZE: Adults 1.8–2.0 m (6–6.6 ft), 75 kg. At birth approx 0.8 m (32 in).

BODY: Fairly robust with moderate keel. **Beak relatively short and broad.** Dark, slender, pointed flippers.

COLOR: Tricolored background: dark gray back, gray sides, and white belly. **Cape dips near eye and below dorsal fin. Black lips, beak tip,** and **snout ridgeline.**

TEETH: Small, sharp, and conical; 86–116 upper row, 86–116 lower row.

DORSAL FIN: Tall, **dark, falcate,** less triangular than spinner.

BEHAVIOR: Gregarious; groups to 50. May bowride. Thought to feed nocturnally.

DIVE PATTERN: Acrobatic: Many make full spins when leaping.

HABITAT: Pelagic and deep waters around oceanic islands. Seaward of continental shelf edge.

DIET: Squid and deepwater fish.

Clymene Dolphin

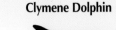

CAN BE CONFUSED WITH:

Common Dolphin

Spinner Dolphin

Atlantic Spotted Dolphin

Clymenes have a moderately short black-tipped beak and smooth-edged cape that dips above eye and below dorsal fin on their tricolored sides.

DISTRIBUTION: Atlantic only. In w. N. Atlantic, seen in winter, spring, and summer in deep waters off n. Gulf of Mexico; strandings n. to NJ.

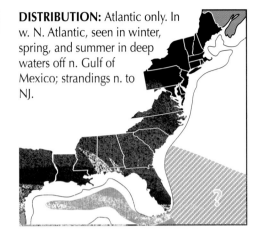

LIFE HISTORY: Unknown.

STATUS AND HUMAN INTERACTIONS: Population status and trend uncertain. Estimated minimum of 5,570 in Gulf of Mexico.

Clymene dolphins have a black ridgeline that runs down their short beak to black lips.

Carol Roden/SEFSC

Keith Mullin/SEFSC

CLYMENE DOLPHIN (Pronounced "cly-MEE-nee")

Other names: short-snouted spinner dolphin

79

<3 m (10 ft)

SIZE: Adults 1.4–1.9 m (4.5–6 ft), 90 kg. At birth approx 0.8 m (32 in).

BODY: Smallest cetacean in U.S. Atlantic. Stocky with small pointed flippers. **No beak.** Small bumps on leading edge of dorsal fin.

COLOR: Dark gray or black on back with lighter sides and white belly. Dark narrow band between mouth and flipper. **No distinctive markings.**

TEETH: Small, spade-like; 40–56 upper row, 40–56 lower row.

DORSAL FIN: Small, triangular; located slightly aft of mid-body.

BEHAVIOR: Travel alone or in groups of 2–10. May approach stationary vessels but generally avoid moving vessels and usually **do not bow-ride.** Not acrobatic.

DIVE PATTERN: Surface frequently when traveling but may take 3–4 breaths at 2–3 min intervals when feeding.

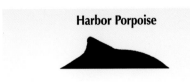

Harbor Porpoise

DISTRIBUTION: N. Hemisphere. In U.S. Atlantic, n. of Cape Hatteras. Seasonal concentrations: spring on Georges Bank and Nantucket Shoals, summer in n. Gulf of Maine and Bay of Fundy, winter in mid-Atlantic.

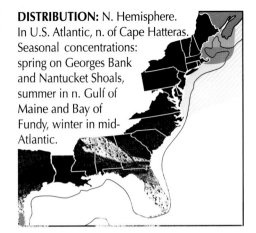

HABITAT: Coastal, cold waters usually less than 200 m (650 ft) deep but may winter off shelf.

DIET: Schooling fish and invertebrates, including herring, mackerel, and squid.

LIFE HISTORY: Sexually mature at 3–5 yrs. Breed in summer. Single calf born every 1+ yrs after gestation of 10–11 mos. Lactation lasts approx 3 mos. May live 13 yrs.

STATUS AND HUMAN INTERACTIONS: Estimated 54,000–74,000 in n. Gulf of Maine and Bay of Fundy in summer. Many are incidentally caught in gillnet fisheries throughout range. Known to carry high levels of contaminants, particularly PCBs and DDT.

Harbor porpoise teeth are spade-shaped (top) while dolphin teeth are sharp and conical (bottom).

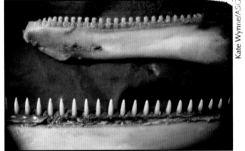

Kate Wynne/ASG

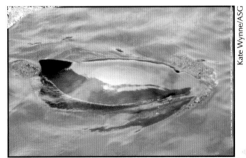

Kate Wynne/ASG

Harbor porpoises have a small, triangular dorsal fin.

HARBOR PORPOISE

<3 m (10 ft)

Other names: puffing pig, common porpoise

81

Seals and manatees are only distantly related mammals (see page 3) that have successfully adapted to a marine existence. Seals belong to one of three families of pinnipeds or "fin-footed" carnivores. Manatees, like their cousin the dugong, are marine herbivores called sirenians or sea cows. This section, therefore, is a convenient, rather than taxonomic, grouping of the few non-cetacean Atlantic marine mammal species.

Pinnipeds

Pinnipeds have adapted to an amphibious marine existence. They forage at sea but come ashore or onto ice at times to rest, give birth, and suckle their young. Many of their anatomical features reflect compromises needed to succeed both on land and in the water. Their large eyes and well-developed whiskers allow feeding in dimly lit water but also function above water. They have webbed flippers and hydrodynamic bodies and appendages for swimming efficiently, but their flippers allow mobility on land as well. They have fur that is molted (shed) annually and a blubber layer for added insulation.

Pinnipeds are carnivores that have retained canine teeth but whose molars are modified for consuming prey whole. Many pinnipeds are capable of long, deep, repetitive dives made possible by physiological traits such as high blood volume and hemoglobin content and a reducible heart rate.

Seals of U.S. Atlantic waters are phocids—members of the pinniped family Phocidae—and are referred to as earless seals because they have no visible external ear flaps (pinnae). Their bodies are spindle-shaped with short necks. On shore or ice, seals use their short, clawed front flippers for traction and extend their hind flippers behind them as they move in a caterpillar-like fashion. Despite their awkward motion on land, they are fast, agile swimmers that propel themselves with an egg beater–like motion of their hind flippers. Phocids breed on land, in the water, or on ice and give birth the following year. Their pups grow rapidly and are weaned abruptly after brief lactation during which their mothers often fast.

Kate Wynne/ASG

Manatees

Manatees are sirenians and are more closely related to elephants than to other marine mammals. They are completely aquatic and herbivorous, feeding on submerged vegetation along tropical coasts, rivers, and estuaries.

Manatees have many unique traits related to their vegetarian lifestyle: prehensile lips and dexterous forelimbs, horny plates inside the front of the mouth, a complex gastrointestinal tract, and molars that are replaced throughout life. Although completely aquatic, they are slow, shallow swimmers that are propelled by a broad, flattened, paddle-like tail (unlike cetacean flukes). They are insulated by blubber but are cold-intolerant and lack numerous marine adaptations found in cetaceans and pinnipeds. Unlike most marine mammals, manatees have a poorly developed adult brain that weighs less than 400 g (less than 1 lb).

Many of the manatees' physical and behavioral traits enhance their exposure to a variety of man-made hazards. They are caught in flood-control gates while feeding in rivers, congregate in the warm outfall of power plants, and are particularly vulnerable to collision with motorboats. Interestingly, unlike other mammals, manatees have elongated lungs that run along an extended length of their backs with the muscular divider (diaphragm) between the lungs and abdominal cavity nearly horizontal. As an unfortunate consequence, much of the back is buoyed as the manatee surfaces to breathe, raising the entire back to within propeller depth.

John Bengtson/NMML

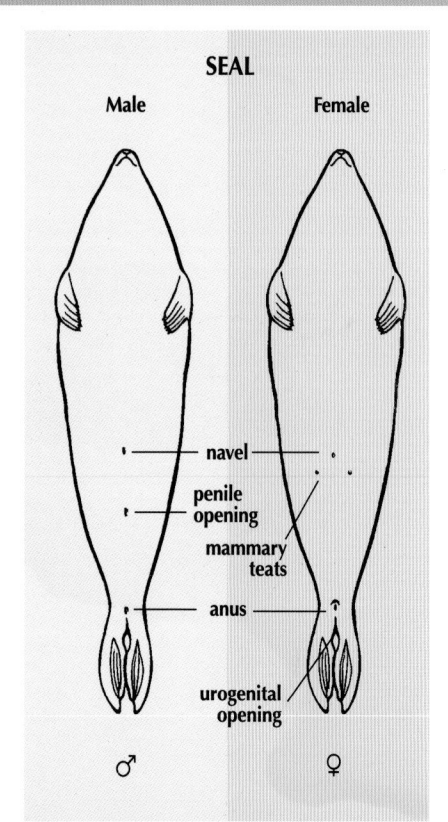

SEAL

Male Female

navel

penile
opening

mammary
teats

anus

urogenital
opening

♂ ♀

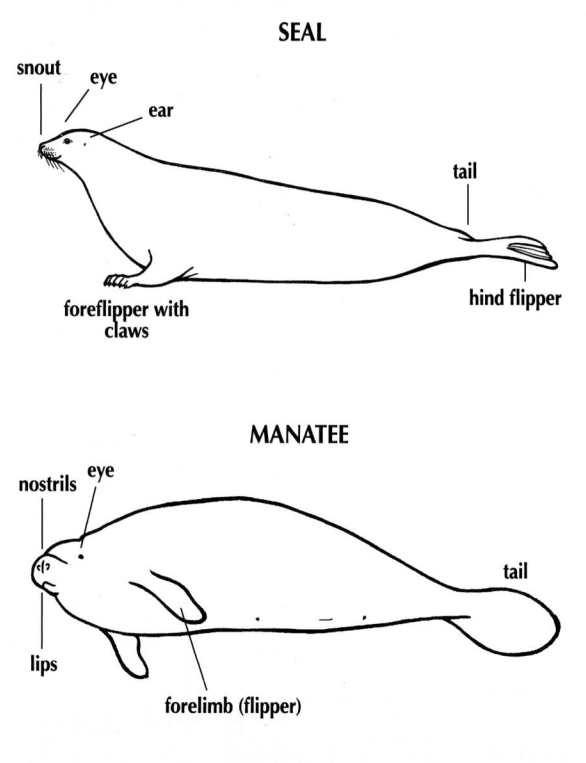

SEAL

snout eye

ear

tail

foreflipper with
claws

hind flipper

MANATEE

nostrils eye

tail

lips

forelimb (flipper)

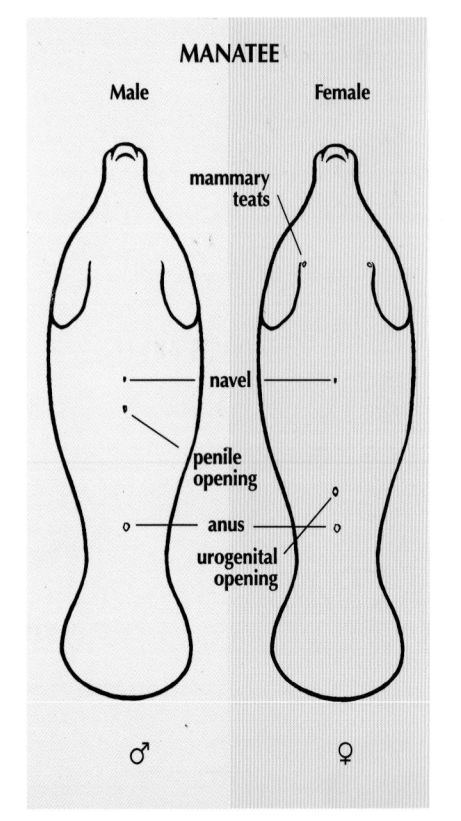

MANATEE

Male Female

mammary
teats

navel

penile
opening

anus

urogenital
opening

♂ ♀

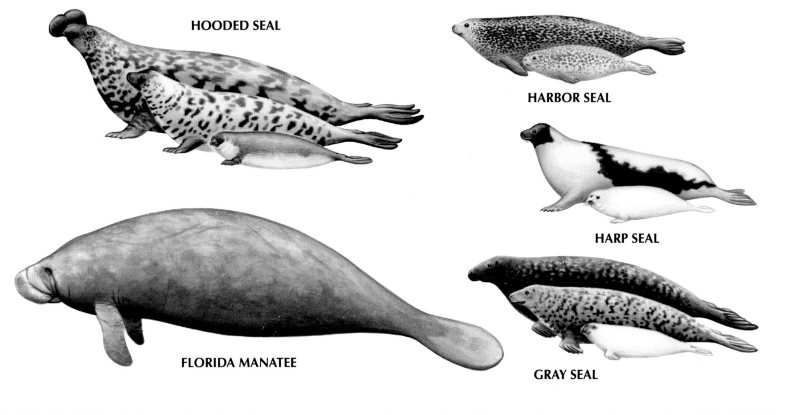

HOODED SEAL

HARBOR SEAL

HARP SEAL

FLORIDA MANATEE

GRAY SEAL

U.S. ATLANTIC SEALS AND MANATEE

85

SIZE: Adults to 1.7–1.9 m (5.6–6.3 ft), 120 kg; males slightly larger than females. At birth approx 0.7 m (30 in), 10 kg.

BODY: Rounded head with short, concave, dog-like snout. Eyes equidistant between ears and nose. Nostrils form "V" when viewed head-on. Sexes similar.

COLOR: Variable: silver to reddish tan to nearly black; often blue-gray back with light and dark speckling, lighter belly. **Pups** usually born with adult-like coat (lanugo is molted in uterus).

BEHAVIOR: Gregarious; few to 100s haul out together. Often lie with head and rear flippers elevated in "banana-like" fashion. Associate with gray seals where ranges overlap.

HABITAT: Temperate, mostly coastal. Use sandy or rocky sites as haulouts and pupping sites. Current U.S. Atlantic pupping occurs only in ME, often on traditionally used protected sites in upper reaches of bays.

Harbor Seal

CAN BE CONFUSED WITH:

Gray Seal

Post-canines (teeth posterior to canines) in lower jaw are multicuspid, overlapping, and angled backward. ▼

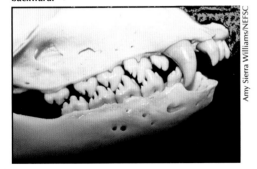

Amy Sierra Williams/NEFSC

DISTRIBUTION: N. Hemisphere. In w. N. Atlantic, range from e. Canada to s. New England. Spring-summer concentration in ME and e. Canada waters; disperse fall-winter and found as far s. as Long Island.

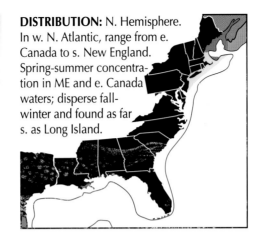

Harbor seals have a short, concave, dog-like snout. ▼

Kate Wynne/ASG

DIET: Variety of schooling fish, groundfish, squid, octopus.

LIFE HISTORY: Sexually mature at 3–6 yrs. Breed May–Jul after pups are weaned. Single pup per yr born Apr–Jun after gestation of 11–12 mos. Lactation lasts 25–30 days. Non-pups molt Jul–Aug. May live 35 yrs.

STATUS AND HUMAN INTERACTIONS: Most common seal in U.S. Atlantic; population increasing—estimated at 29,000–35,000. Perceived conflicts with commercial fisheries led to a bounty in New England until late 1960s. Incidentally caught in gillnets and other fixed-gear fisheries.

Their smaller size and dog-like profile help distinguish harbor seals from gray seals. ▼

Bob Bowman/CCS-Maine

HARBOR SEAL

Other names: common seal, hair seal

SIZE: Adult males to 2.3 m (7.5 ft), 300 kg. Adult females to 2.0 m (6.6 ft),180 kg. At birth approx 1 m (3 ft), 20 kg.

BODY: Distinctive horse-like head with broad arching snout. Eyes set closer to ears than nose. Nostrils form "W". Sexually dimorphic: adult males much larger than females, with thicker neck, broader head, and darker pelage.

COLOR: Adults darker on back than belly; colors range from black, tan, silver, to white. Generally **males are dark with irregular light patches** and **females are light with dark spots. Pups:** born with lanugo (white or yellowish) and molt to spotted coat at 2–4 wks.

BEHAVIOR: Gregarious; form large rookeries during pupping, molting, breeding seasons. Polygynous breeders, but males do not defend territories or harems. Associate with harbor seals where ranges overlap.

HABITAT: Temperate to subarctic. Use sandy or rocky sites exposed to rough seas and riptides as haulouts and pupping rookeries. Mostly pelagic for first few yrs of life.

Gray Seal

CAN BE CONFUSED WITH:
Ice Seals and

Harbor Seal

All post-canines are sharp and canine-like on gray seals. ▼

Amy Sierra Williams/NEFSC

DISTRIBUTION: N. Atlantic only. W. N. Atlantic population centered in e. Canada but range to s. New England. Seasonal movements but no well-defined migration.

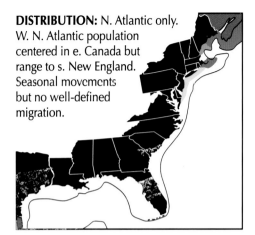

Paul Thompson/UAUK

◄ Gray seal pups share their parents' "horsehead" profile and are born with yellow or white lanugo.

DIET: Variety of schooling fish, squid, octopus. Newly weaned pups eat shrimp and crabs. Adults fast during breeding season.

LIFE HISTORY: Females sexually mature at 3–5 yrs, males at 4–8 yrs. Breed in winter after pups are weaned. Single pup per yr born on land or ice in Dec–Feb after gestation of 11–12 mos. Lactation lasts 16–17 days. Non-pups molt from Mar–Jun. May live 30–50 yrs.

STATUS AND HUMAN INTERACTIONS: Population increasing with estimated 143,000 in e. Canada. A growing number (approx 3,000 in 1993) are pupping and molting on ME and MA sites. Perceived conflicts with commercial fisheries, including concerns about codworm infestation, led to Canadian bounty and culling of ±2,000 per yr from 1967–83. Incidentally caught in some fixed-gear fisheries.

GRAY SEAL

HOODED SEAL

SIZE: Adult males 2.3–2.7 m (7.5–9 ft), 375 kg. Adult females 2.0–2.2 m (6.5–7 ft), 300 kg. At birth approx 1 m (3.3 ft), 15 kg.

BODY: Large body with relatively **broad, flattened head.** Adult **males** larger than females and **have inflatable sac ("hood") on top of nose and forehead.**

COLOR: Adults: **blue-gray with irregular black blotches, black face,** and light belly. **Pups: blue-gray back and face** and contrasting light belly (called "blue-backs").

BEHAVIOR: Males can inflate and shake their hood and extrude a **red balloon-like membrane** from left nostril, often in aggressive or defensive displays. Usually solitary but gather as triads (bull, cow, and pup) during breeding season. Highly migratory; common for adults and juveniles to wander beyond normal range.

HABITAT: Prefer deep offshore waters and thick drifting ice floes.

DIET: Variety of fish, squid, shrimp, octopus. Most adults fast during pupping and molting seasons.

Hooded Seal

CAN BE CONFUSED WITH:

Harp Seal

DISTRIBUTION: N. Atlantic only; primarily n. of Gulf of St. Lawrence. May stray s. into U.S. waters (to FL) Dec–Mar. Migrate n. from winter pupping-breeding areas to molt off Greenland dispersing n. and e. to feed in summer.

LIFE HISTORY: Females sexually mature at 3–5 yrs, males at 4–6 yrs. Breed in Apr after pups are weaned. Single pup per yr born Mar–Apr after gestation of 11–12 mos. Lactation lasts 4 days—the shortest known for any mammal. Non-pups molt Jun–Aug. May live 30 yrs.

STATUS AND HUMAN INTERACTIONS: Population apparently increasing; approx 400,000 in e. Canada. No estimate for number using U.S. waters, but frequency of strandings has increased. Commercially harvested in e. Canada until 1980s, often secondary to harp seal harvests.

Hooded seals have blunt, star-shaped post-canines. ▼

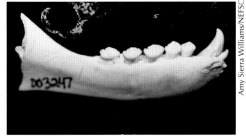

Amy Sierra Williams/NEFSC

A young hooded seal, or "blue-back," has a broader and flatter head than a harbor or harp seal. ▼

Graham Worthy/TAMU

In addition to displaying their inflatable "hood," male hooded seals may extrude a red "balloon" from their left nostril. ▼

Graham Worthy/TAMU

HOODED SEAL

Other names: crested seal, bladdernose seal

SIZE: Adults to 1.7–1.9 m (5.6–6.3 ft),180 kg; males slightly larger than females. At birth approx 0.9 m (2.5–3 ft), 10 kg.

BODY: Robust body with relatively **small, sleek** head. Well-developed claws on front flippers.

COLOR: Adults: silver-gray body with black face and wishbone-shaped "harp" on back (often muted or covered by large blotches on females). **Pups:** born with yellowish lanugo that becomes "white-coat" after 3 days; molt into black-spotted silvery coat at 4 wks (as "beaters"). Year-old "bedlamers" molt into an irregularly blotched coat that develops into adult harp pattern with each annual molt.

BEHAVIOR: Pagophilic (ice-associated) and highly migratory. Gregarious: 10,000s congregate on pupping and molting grounds, 100s migrate, rest, and feed together in summer.

HABITAT: Closely associated with shore-fast sea ice. Have pups, breed, and spend winter on pack ice; follow receding sea ice n. in spring to feed.

Harp Seal

CAN BE CONFUSED WITH:

Hooded Seal

Harbor Seal

DISTRIBUTION: N. Hemisphere. In w. N. Atlantic, primarily n. of Gulf of St. Lawrence but juveniles range s. into U.S. waters (to NJ) in Jan–May when population is at s. limit of its migration.

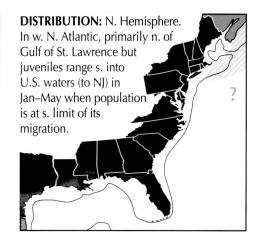

DIET: Crustaceans, groundfish, schooling fish. Juveniles eat shrimp-like crustaceans. Most fast while molting.

LIFE HISTORY: Sexually mature at 4–7 yrs. Breed in Mar after pups are weaned. Single pup per yr born Feb–Mar after gestation of 11–12 mos. Lactation lasts 12 days. Non-pups molt early Apr. May live 30 yrs.

STATUS AND HUMAN INTERACTIONS: Estimated 3–5 million in N. Atlantic and increasing. No estimate available for increasing number of juveniles seen in U.S. waters. Commercially hunted in e. Canada since mid-1800s; 53,000–95,000 per yr were taken from 1988–92 in government-set harvest. Incidentally caught in gillnets.

Post-canines in lower jaw are tricuspid, evenly spaced, and shark-like. ▶

Right: Most harp seals seen in U.S. waters are juveniles that have large irregular blotches on their dark-over-light coats.

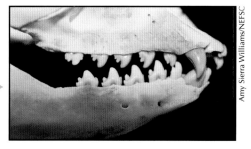

Amy Sierra Williams/NEFSC

Graham Worthy/TAMU

HARP SEAL

Other names: Greenland seal, saddle-back seal

SIZE: Adults 2.5–4.5 m (8.2–14.8 ft), to 1,600 kg. At birth approx 1 m (3.3 ft), 30 kg.

BODY: Rotund body with relatively small head and no neck crease. **Prominent bristly muzzle with prehensile lips.** Tail large and spatulate. Long dexterous forelimbs (pectoral flippers) have nails on squared outer edges and a single nipple at their base. **Eyes are small and deeply set.**

COLOR: Uniformly gray or gray-brown. Blotches and scarring from boat propellers are common.

TEETH: Molars are continuously shed from front and replaced from rear; 6–12 lower row, 6–12 upper row.

BEHAVIOR: Docile and often curious, approachable, and playful. Group together at sources of warm water during cold weather. Make extensive (up to 1,700 km round-trip) seasonal inshore-offshore or n.-s. movements in response to temperature change. Generally slow swimmers but capable of short bursts of speed. Avg dives 4 min, max dives 24 min.

DISTRIBUTION: Tropical
Atlantic in U.S. waters,
primarily Fl. and
se. GA, but range from
TX on Gulf Coast to
NJ or

Florida Manatee

John Bengtson/NMML

DISTRIBUTION: Tropical w. Atlantic. In U.S. waters, primarily peninsular FL and s.e. GA, but range from TX on Gulf Coast n. as far as RI.

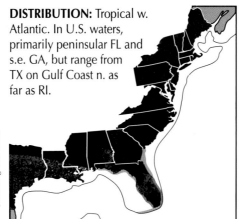

When manatees surface to breathe, they are particularly vulnerable to motorboat strikes, as evidenced by propeller scars on most animals.

Manatees use their dexterous forelimbs and prehensile lips to feed on water plants. ▶

John Bengtson/NMML

HABITAT: Warm coastal and inland waters. Found in marine, estuarine, and riverine waters, but need access to freshwater. Often congregate in warm springs and near power-plant outfalls during cold weather. Low tolerance to water temps less than 20°C (68°F).

DIET: Herbivorous; submerged vegetation, seagrasses, floating or emergent plants. Captive manatees eat up to 75 kg of vegetation daily.

LIFE HISTORY: Sexually mature at 3–5 yrs. May breed year-round. Single calf (rarely twins) every 2–5 yrs after gestation of approx 12 mos, usually born in quiet waters and canals. Lactation lasts 1–2 yrs. May live to 60 yrs.

STATUS AND HUMAN INTERACTIONS: Endangered but stable; only 2,229 counted in FL in 1997. Boat collisions, crushing in flood-control structures, cold-stress, and toxic algal blooms are known to be significant sources of mortality. Vulnerable to coastal development and industrial catastrophes.

FLORIDA MANATEE

Other names: sea cow, manatee, West Indian manatee

Unlike all the other animals in this book, sea turtles are reptiles—taxonomically distant and distinct from marine mammals. They have dry, scaly skin, which is relatively impermeable to water; are ectothermic; and like many reptiles, lay eggs. The most distinguishing characteristic of sea turtles is their shell, a defining trait they share with all turtles. From terrestrial ancestors, marine turtles evolved secondarily to a marine existence. This resulted in a strongly tapered, streamlined shell and powerful, rigid, paddle-like forelimbs that "fly" through the water with amazing speed, without compromising the ability to move on land—an inescapable confine for animals that must come ashore to lay their eggs.

Strong swimmers, sea turtles are capable of making deep, repetitive dives to search for food and can remain submerged for long periods of time, such as when resting on the ocean bottom. In fact, sea turtles spend little time at the water surface—often just long enough to take a breath of air—though some sea turtles, such as the leatherback and loggerhead, can be found basking at the water surface. Basking in the sun may aid in maintaining a body temperature higher than that of the surrounding water, allowing for survival in colder Atlantic waters.

Life History

Sea turtles migrate, sometimes long distances, from foraging grounds to shallow-water nesting grounds to mate, nest, and lay their eggs. The female emerges from the water and digs a flask-shaped nest in the sand with her hind flippers, then lays 50 to 170 (depending on the species) ping-pong ball–shaped eggs. After covering the nest with sand, she returns to the water. She will nest several times in one season. After the nesting season, she migrates back to the foraging grounds. In most species of sea turtles, mature females do not nest every year, remaining instead at the foraging grounds in off years.

Following an 8-to-10-week incubation, the eggs hatch, and the hatchlings dig their way out of the nest, usually emerging at night. They make their way to the water, orienting themselves to the brightest horizon (hatchlings disoriented by brightly lit beaches become more vulnerable to hazards such as predation and dessication). Once in the water, they swim rapidly—"swimming frenzy"—until they reach the open ocean, where many species spend the "lost years" living and feeding in floating sargassum. They "reappear" as juveniles in feeding grounds shared with adults or, in some cases, migrate to developmental feeding grounds. But some species, such as the leatherback, spend their entire lives in a pelagic existence, coming inshore only to mate and nest.

Courtesy of CEE

Conservation

Probably the single greatest threat to sea turtle survival in U.S. Atlantic waters is entanglement in active and discarded fishing gear. Sea turtles that become entangled and cannot reach the surface to breathe become increasingly anoxic (oxygen depleted) and comatose. Not all turtles in this condition are dead. Although they are inactive and their heart rate is negligible, recent research shows that they may be able to recover.

You can help sea turtles found in this condition: Place the turtle in the shade, carapace-up, and keep it moist with seawater until flipper activity resumes. Recovery may take more than 2 hours. Remember: Regulations require that you return the turtle to the water.

Dermochelyidae

Carapace and plastron lack horny shell scutes, being covered instead by leathery skin. Underlying bones of the shell are almost completely lost, their place taken by a mosaic of thousands of tiny bones imbedded below the leathery skin. Forelimbs are smooth, broad, and paddle-like and lack claws. This family is represented by a single living species, *Dermochelys coriacea*, the leatherback sea turtle.

Cheloniidae

Family composed of the "hard-shelled" sea turtles. Shell is covered with horny scutes, variable in number, but usually including 5 vertebral scutes, 4 or 5 pairs of costal scutes, and 3 or 4 pairs of inframarginal scutes. Carapace is oval to heart-shaped. Forelimbs are covered with scales, are paddle-like, with elongated digits and 1 to 2 claws on each forelimb.

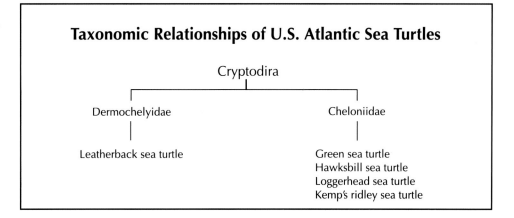

Taxonomic Relationships of U.S. Atlantic Sea Turtles

Cryptodira

- Dermochelyidae
  - Leatherback sea turtle
- Cheloniidae
  - Green sea turtle
  - Hawksbill sea turtle
  - Loggerhead sea turtle
  - Kemp's ridley sea turtle

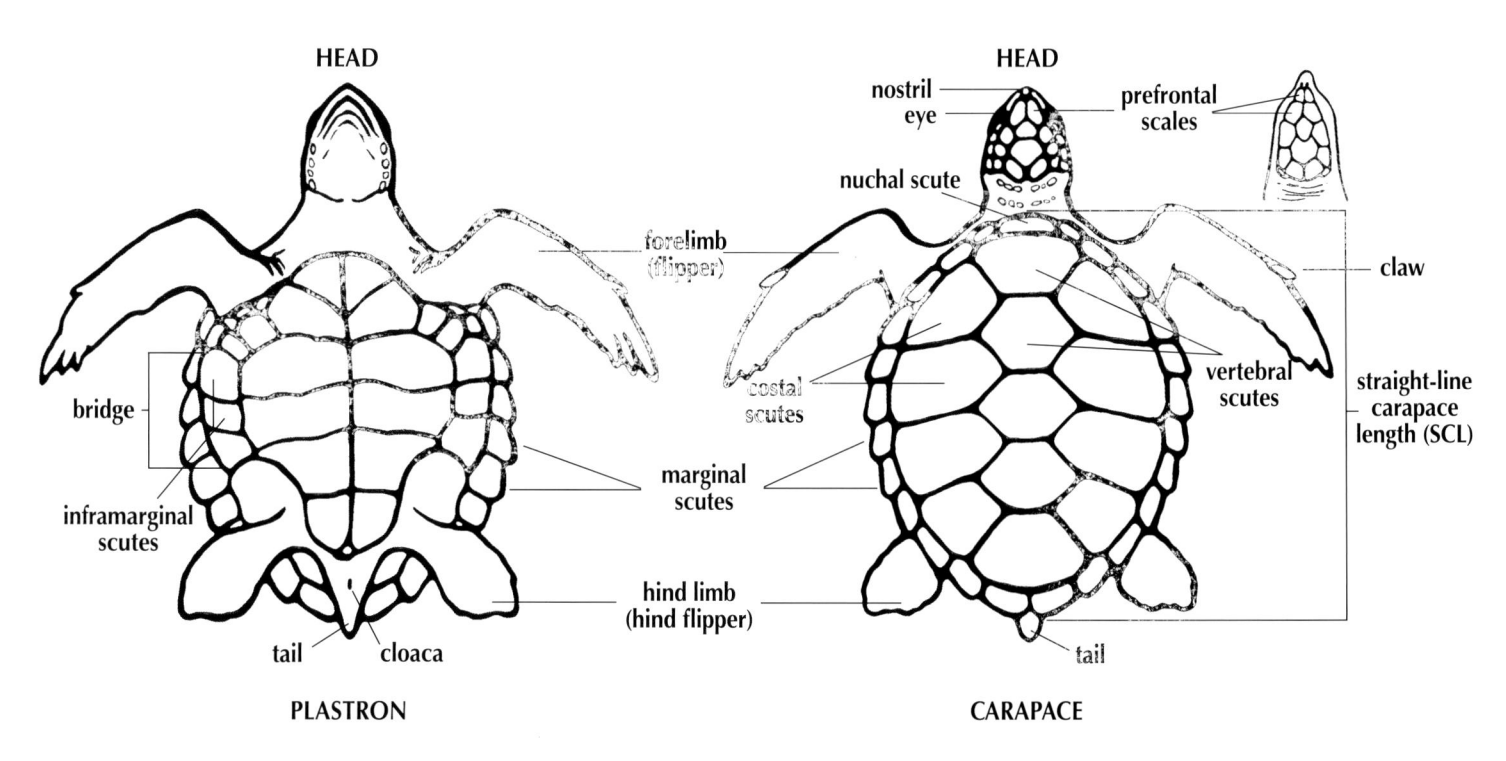

HEAD

HEAD

nostril
eye

prefrontal
scales

nuchal scute

forelimb
(flipper)

claw

bridge

costal
scutes

vertebral
scutes

straight-line
carapace
length (SCL)

inframarginal
scutes

marginal
scutes

hind limb
(hind flipper)

tail   cloaca

tail

PLASTRON

CARAPACE

Note: Sex of sea turtles is difficult to determine through external morphology.

HAWKSBILL SEA TURTLE

KEMP'S RIDLEY SEA TURTLE

GREEN SEA TURTLE

LEATHERBACK SEA TURTLE

LOGGERHEAD SEA TURTLE

U.S. ATLANTIC SEA TURTLES

99

SIZE: Adult shell to 1.8 m SCL (6 ft), 727 kg to 1 ton.

BODY/SHELL: Largest living turtle. **Lacks shell scutes, head and body scales.** Covered by **leathery skin.** Carapace divided longitudinally by 7 ridges; hingeless plastron divided by 5 ridges; head short, blunt, with **2 cusps projecting from upper jaw.** Limbs **clawless.**

COLOR: Only black marine turtle in Atlantic, but often spotted with white or pinkish blue on undersides of head, limbs, body.

BEHAVIOR: Solitary at sea, but adults may congregate off nesting beaches or while feeding on jellyfish. Relatively fast swimmers (>10 knots), breach occasionally. Spend majority of time feeding or basking near or at water surface. Most dives <200 m (660 ft), <20 min; but can dive to 1,300 m (4,290 ft).

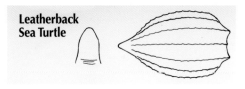
Leatherback Sea Turtle

DISTRIBUTION: Worldwide. In w. N. Atlantic, from Gulf of Mexico and Caribbean to Iceland. Migrate n. in summer along Gulf Stream. Found n. of Cape Hatteras from Jun–Oct. Likely winter from FL and Caribbean south.

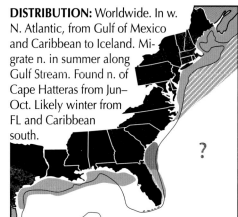

?

HABITAT: Highly pelagic, migratory. Occasionally enter shallow waters of bays and estuaries.

DIET: Primarily jellyfish.

LIFE HISTORY: Courtship and mating thought to occur off nesting beaches. In w. Atlantic, nesting occurs Apr–Nov on e. coast of FL, Caribbean, and s.; rarely in TX, GA, SC, NC. Mature females may oviposit >6 times per year, laying 50–170 eggs per clutch. Incubation lasts 53–74 days. Little is known about hatchling, juvenile movements.

Right photo: The leatherback lacks a bony shell. Instead, the shell is covered by a thin, black, leathery skin raised in 7 ridges.

The two cusps on the upper jaw of a leatherback assist in grasping slippery jellyfish prey. ▼

STATUS AND HUMAN INTERACTIONS: Endangered. Principal threats in U.S. Atlantic are entanglement in fixed fishing gear, boat collisions, debris ingestion. Threats to eggs and hatchlings include nesting beach alteration and artificial lighting.

Larry Wood/MCJB

Scott Kraus/NEA

NOTE: Mortality of marine turtles found entangled/entrapped can be reduced: Place turtle carapace-up; keep moist and in shade until flipper activity resumes.

LEATHERBACK SEA TURTLE

Other names: Luth, leathery turtle

GREEN SEA TURTLE

SIZE: Avg adult shell 1 m SCL (3.3 ft); avg weight 150 kg.

BODY/SHELL: Largest hard-shelled sea turtle. **Carapace smooth,** heart-shaped or oval, covered with horny scutes, with **4 pairs costals, nuchal scute not touching first costal. Head relatively small, rounded, with 1 pair prefrontals.** One claw on each forelimb.

COLOR: Carapace and head olive to brown, some with mottled, radiating, or wavy pattern on scutes; plastron yellowish white. Hatchlings black above, white below.

BEHAVIOR: Can migrate great distances from nesting beaches to foraging grounds.

HABITAT: Pelagic as hatchlings (to 0.25 m SCL), then move to benthic feeding grounds; juveniles and adults congregate in relatively shallow, protected waters containing seagrass, macroalgae "pastures"; also coral reefs, worm reefs, rocky bottoms.

Green Sea Turtle

CAN BE CONFUSED WITH:

Hawksbill Sea Turtle

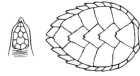

Loggerhead Sea Turtle

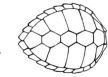

Kemp's Ridley Sea Turtle

Greens can be distinguished by their smooth carapace and only 1 pair of prefrontal scales between the eyes. Note that carapace color is highly variable. ▶

DISTRIBUTION: Worldwide. In w. Atlantic, range from MA to Argentina, including Gulf of Mexico and Caribbean. Rare n. of Cape I latteras. Migrate seasonally great distances between feeding and nesting areas.

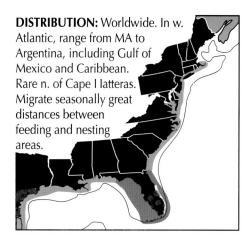

Tom Doty/CETAP

DIET: Pelagic-stage hatchlings and juveniles eat molluscs, jellyfish, crustaceans. Diet shifts to seagrasses, macroalgae as juveniles mature and move inshore.

LIFE HISTORY: Mating occurs off nesting beaches close to shore. Mature females nest Mar–Oct (peak May–Jun). U.S. nesting occurs on tropical beaches in FL, Puerto Rico, U.S. Virgin Islands. Females oviposit avg 2–3 times per season, laying 100–150 eggs per clutch. Incubation lasts 45–60 days.

STATUS AND HUMAN INTERACTIONS: Breeding population endangered in FL; threatened elsewhere. Historically exploited for eggs, meat. In U.S. Atlantic, degradation of nesting and feeding habitats, boat collisions, fishing gear entanglement, and disease are serious problems.

NOTE: Mortality of marine turtles found entangled/entrapped can be reduced: Place turtle carapace-up; keep moist and in shade until flipper activity resumes.

GREEN SEA TURTLE

Other names: edible turtle

LOGGERHEAD SEA TURTLE

Carretta carretta
Family: Cheloniidae

SIZE: Avg adult shell 0.92 m SCL (3 ft), can reach 1.2 m; avg adult weight 115 kg.

BODY/SHELL: Carapace covered with horny scutes, with **5 pairs costals, nuchal scute touches first costal; 3 pairs inframarginals present on bridge.** Head large, broad, with 2 pairs prefrontals; jaws powerful for crushing prey. Two claws on each forelimb.

COLOR: Carapace and head yellow-orange to reddish brown, often covered by barnacles, fouling organisms; plastron yellowish to light brown. Hatchlings light brown to almost black.

BEHAVIOR: Hatchlings engage in "swimming frenzy" for about 20 hrs after hatching, carrying them offshore. May live in sargassum rafts until they reach approx 0.45 m SCL. Juveniles, adults tend to congregate at same nearshore feeding grounds each year. Loggerheads may hibernate in winter.

HABITAT: Pelagic as hatchlings, then migrate to nearshore waters. Adults, juveniles inhabit subtropical continental shelf and coastal waters (bays, lagoons, river mouths).

Loggerhead Sea Turtle

CAN BE CONFUSED WITH:

Kemp's Ridley Sea Turtle

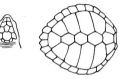

Hawksbill Sea Turtle

Green Sea Turtle

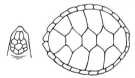

Loggerheads have a large, broad head and often have fouling organisms, such as barnacles, on the shell and body. ▶

DISTRIBUTION: Worldwide. In w. Atlantic, from Newfoundland to Argentina, including Gulf of Mexico and Caribbean. Migrate n. over continental shelf in summer; found n. of Cape Hatteras May–Oct. Retreat s. in winter.

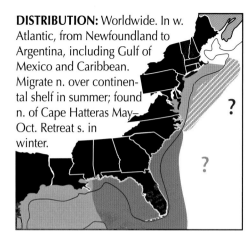

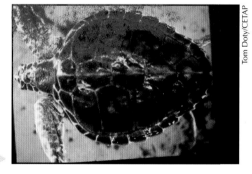

Tom Doty/CETAP

DIET: Primarily benthic feeders on crustaceans, molluscs.

LIFE HISTORY: Sexes thought to migrate together from foraging sites to nesting beaches, where mating occurs in surface waters. Nest Apr–Sep (peak Jun–Jul) on temperate beaches from s. NJ to FL; major U.S. nesting area is e. FL. Mature females may oviposit 3–6 times per season, laying 95–150 eggs per clutch. Incubation lasts 49–71 days.

STATUS AND HUMAN INTERACTIONS: Threatened. In U.S. Atlantic, greatest known mortality is entanglement in towed or fixed fishing gear. Boat collisions are also a serious problem. Threats to eggs, hatchlings include nesting beach degradation (development, erosion control, etc.) and artificial lighting.

NOTE: Mortality of marine turtles found entangled/entrapped can be reduced: Place turtle carapace-up; keep moist and in shade until flipper activity resumes.

LOGGERHEAD SEA TURTLE

HAWKSBILL SEA TURTLE

Eretmochelys imbricata
Family: Cheloniidae

106

SIZE: Avg adult shell 0.66–0.86 m SCL (2.2–2.8 ft); avg weight 82 kg.

BODY/SHELL: Carapace shield-shaped, covered with **thick, horny, overlapping scutes, with 4 pairs costals, nuchal scute not touching first costal.** Head narrow with 2 pairs prefrontals, **beak-like snout. Two claws on each** forelimb.

COLOR: Carapace pattern "tortoiseshell," with radiating brown, black, amber streaks; head scales dark brown with yellow margins; plastron yellow.

BEHAVIOR: Migrate between feeding and nesting grounds. Adults, large juveniles capable of making deep dives (>100 m) to forage on deepwater sponges.

HABITAT: Pelagic as hatchlings and juveniles (to 0.25 m SCL), then move to feeding grounds in rocky or coral reef waters in the tropics, subtropics. Pelagic and benthic habitats poorly understood. Juveniles favor shallow waters, adults may forage in deeper waters.

**Hawksbill
Sea Turtle**

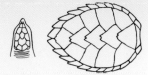

CAN BE CONFUSED WITH:

**Green
Sea Turtle**

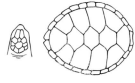

**Loggerhead
Sea Turtle**

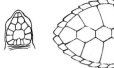

**Kemp's Ridley
Sea Turtle**

DISTRIBUTION: Worldwide, primarily tropics. In w. Atlantic, range from MA to Brazil, including Gulf of Mexico and Caribbean. Rare n. of VA.

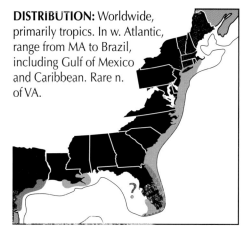

DIET: Primarily sponges and benthic invertebrates.

LIFE HISTORY: Nesting occurs year-round. In w. Atlantic, nest on beaches in Caribbean, C. and S. America. Rare nesting in FL. Mature females oviposit avg 4–6 times per season, laying 140–160 eggs per clutch. Incubation lasts 47–77 days.

STATUS AND HUMAN INTERACTIONS: Endangered. Highly exploited worldwide for tortoiseshell, and more recently, whole stuffed turtles. In U.S. Atlantic and Caribbean, degradation of coral reefs and nesting beaches remains a serious problem.

NOTE: Mortality of marine turtles found entangled/entrapped can be reduced: Place turtle carapace-up; keep moist and in shade until flipper activity resumes.

Rob Nawojchik/MA

The bird-like "beak" of the hawksbill aids in feeding from crevices and hard surfaces, such as coral reefs.

HAWKSBILL SEA TURTLE

SIZE: Smallest sea turtle; adult shell 0.58–0.80 m SCL (1.9–2.6 ft); weight 40–50 kg.

BODY/SHELL: Carapace heart-shaped, covered with horny scutes, with **5 costals, nuchal scute touches first costal; 4 inframarginals with pores present on bridge.** Head broad, but pointed, with 2 pairs prefrontals; jaws powerful and strongly ridged. One claw on each forelimb.

COLOR: Carapace light olive to gray; head and limbs gray; plastron white. Hatchlings dark gray to black.

BEHAVIOR: Adults found at feeding grounds primarily in the Gulf of Mexico. Juveniles feed in nearshore waters along the East Coast and Gulf; migrate s. for winter. Some remain too long, are caught in cold water, become cold-stunned, and die.

HABITAT: Pelagic as hatchlings (to 0.20 m SCL), then enter nearshore waters, primarily those with seagrass beds or mud bottoms favored by crabs. Adults, juveniles utilize similar inshore coastal waters.

Kemp's Ridley Sea Turtle

CAN BE CONFUSED WITH:

Loggerhead Sea Turtle

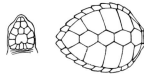

Hawksbill Sea Turtle

Green Sea Turtle

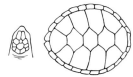

The smallest sea turtle, Kemp's ridley can be distinguished by a heart-shaped carapace and a large, broad head. ▶

DISTRIBUTION: Atlantic, primarily w. N. Atlantic. Range: Nova Scotia to Mexico. Adults and juveniles found year-round in Gulf of Mexico; many juveniles migrate n. along the East Coast in summer, then retreat s. in fall.

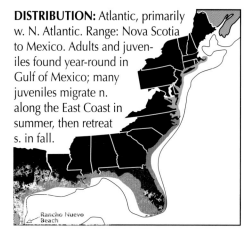

Rancho Nuevo Beach

Tom Doty/CETAP

DIET: Primarily crabs but also shrimp, molluscs.

LIFE HISTORY: Both sexes migrate to waters off nesting beaches to mate. Ridleys are unique: Females may nest in mass aggregations called "arribadas" (Spanish for "arrival"); they nest during the day; and 99% of all nesting occurs on several beaches near Rancho Nuevo, Mexico. Some single nesting occurs on beaches in Mexico, TX, FL, SC, NC. Nest Apr–Aug (peak Apr–Jun) and oviposit avg 3 times per season, laying avg 103 eggs per clutch. Incubation lasts 48–65 days.

STATUS AND HUMAN INTERACTIONS: Endangered. Egg collection, taking of nesting females, and entanglement in towed fishing gear have decimated the species. Mexican and U.S. law now prohibits taking of eggs and turtles. Entanglement in trawls remains the primary source of mortality despite TED regulations.

NOTE: Mortality of marine turtles found entangled/entrapped can be reduced: Place turtle carapace-up; keep moist and in shade until flipper activity resumes.

KEMP'S RIDLEY SEA TURTLE

Other names: Atlantic ridley, Mexican ridley, riddler, bastard turtle, grey loggerhead

The following terms are defined as used in this book (see also morphology diagrams that accompany each section).

Baleen: Bony material formed into comb-like plates, grows from upper jaw of mysticete whales.

Benthic: Associated with the ocean bottom.

Blaze: Pale streak of color, often extending into cape.

Blow: Moist air forcefully exhaled from lungs and through blowhole of a surfacing cetacean.

Bowride: To swim in the wave made by a moving boat, often at the bow or front of the boat.

Breach: To jump clear of the water surface.

Bridge: Series of scutes joining the two halves of a turtle's shell (p. 98).

Callosities: Fleshy wartlike growths from skin of some whales.

Cape: Darker region on back of some cetaceans, around dorsal fin.

Carapace: Bony shield composing the back (dorsal) shell of a turtle (p. 98).

Carnivore: Flesh eater, member of the taxonomic order Carnivora.

Cetacean: Whale, dolphin, or porpoise; member of the taxonomic order Cetacea.

Chevron: V-shaped stripes.

Cloaca: Common cavity into which genital, urinary, and intestinal tracts discharge.

Clutch: A nest of eggs.

Coastal: Adjacent to ocean shore.

Copepod: Small crustacean in the class Copepoda.

Costal scutes: Series of scutes lying along each side of the vertebral scutes on the turtle carapace (p. 98).

Depleted Status: Species whose numbers are below its optimal sustainable population level.

Dimorphism: Two different forms or traits. Sexual dimorphism: traits differ between sexes.

Dive pattern: Typical behavior and timing of a whale's blow and dives.

Ectothermic: Body temperature not physiologically regulated (mimics the environmental temperature).

Endangered Status: Species in danger of extinction in all or significant portion of its range, as defined by the Endangered Species Act.

Endothermic: Body temperature is physiologically regulated (usually maintained at a warm set-point).

Euphausiid: Small shrimp-like crustacean in the order Euphausiacea. Also called krill.

Falcate: Hooked or curved like a sickle.

Flukes: Horizontally flattened cetacean tail (p. 8).

Gestation: The carrying of young in the uterus until birth.

Gregarious: Social.

Hatchling: A recently hatched turtle.

Haulout (noun): A shoreside resting site.

Haul out (verb): To rest onshore.

Herbivorous: Feeding on plants.

Inframarginal scutes: Scutes forming the bridge of a turtle's shell (p. 98).

Keel: Distinctive bulge on one or both sides of the tail stock (p. 8).

Krill: Small, shrimp-like crustaceans (see Euphausiid).

Lactation: Production of milk by female; duration of suckling.

Lanugo: White fur coat that some seal pups are born with or shed just prior to birth.

Lobtail: To forcefully slap water surface with tail.

Logging: Resting motionless at or near water surface.

Melon: Bulbous forehead of toothed whales; believed to help focus sound while echolocating (p. 8).

Molt (noun): Period of time when fur is replaced.

Molt (verb): To shed and replace fur.

Nuchal scute: Scute lying at the anterior midline of the carapace at the base of the head (p. 98).

Oviposit: To lay eggs.

Pack ice: Mass of broken ice pieces, at edge of permanent sea ice.

Pectoral fin: Flipper (p. 8).

Pelagic: Related to deep, open ocean water.

Pinniped: "Fin-footed" carnivores, including seals, sea lions, and walrus.

Plastron: Bony shield composing the lower half of a turtle's shell (p. 98).

Polygynous: One male mates with more than one female.

Porpoising: Leaping above water surface while swimming fast.

Pupping: Process of giving birth in pinnipeds.

Rookery: Land site used by pinnipeds for pupping and breeding.

Rostrum: Upper jaw (p. 8).

Sargassum: A mass of floating vegetation composed largely of a type of brown algae, *Sargassum*.

Scute: Horny scales (plates) that cover underlying bony plates of carapace and plastron (p. 98).

Sexual maturity: Age at which animal is first capable of breeding.

Spyhop: Poke head vertically out of water.

Straight-line carapace length: Horizontal length of a turtle's upper shell from nuchal scute to last vertebral scute, using calipers.

Taxonomy: Classification of organisms according to how they are related to one another.

TED: Turtle excluder device; a grate-like "door" inserted in a fishing net to deflect turtles out of the net.

Threatened Status: Species likely to become endangered within foreseeable future in all or significant part of its range.

Vertebral scutes: Series of scutes lying along the midline of the turtle carapace (p. 98).

Warm-core ring: Body of warm water isolated from Gulf Stream and surrounded by cooler northern water (p. 4).

Zooplankton: Minute animals adrift in water column, including early life stages of fish and invertebrates.

Abbreviations	
approx	approximately
avg	average
cm	centimeter
e.	east, eastern
fa	fathom (equals 6 ft or 1.83 m)
ft	feet
in	inch, inches
kg	kilogram
lb	pounds
m	meter
max	maximum
min	minimum
mo(s)	month(s)
n.	north, northern
s.	south, southern
SCL	straight-line carapace length
sec	seconds
w.	west, western
♂	male
♀	female

TERMS USED IN THIS GUIDE

Marine Mammals:

Gaskin, D.E. 1982. *The Ecology of Whales and Dolphins*. Heinemann, London. 459pp.

Geraci, J.R. and V.J. Lounsbury. 1993. *Marine Mammals Ashore: A Field Guide for Strandings*. Texas Sea Grant, Texas A&M University, College Station, Texas. TAMU-SG-93-601. 305pp.

Jefferson, T.A., S. Leatherwood, L.K.M. Shoda, and R.L. Pitman. 1992. *Marine Mammals of the Gulf of Mexico: A Field Guide for Aerial and Shipboard Observers*. Texas A&M University Printing Center, College Station, Texas. 92pp.

Klinowska, M. 1991. *Dolphins, Porpoises, and Whales of the World: IUCN Red Data Book*. IUCN, Gland, Switzerland and Cambridge, U.K. 429pp.

Leatherwood, S., D.K. Caldwell, and H.E. Winn. 1976. *Whales, Dolphins, and Porpoises of the Western North Atlantic: A Guide to Their Identification*. NOAA Technical Report NMFS CIRC-396. Washington, D.C. 176pp.

Leatherwood, S. and R.R. Reeves. 1983. *The Sierra Club Handbook of Whales and Dolphins*. Sierra Club Books, San Francisco, Calif. 302pp.

Reidman, M. 1990. *The Pinnipeds: Seals, Sea Lions, and Walruses*. University of California Press, Berkeley, Calif. 439pp.

Rice, D.W. 1998. *Marine Mammals of the World, Systematics and Distribution*. Special Publication No. 4. Society for Marine Mammalogy, Lawrence, Kan. 231pp.

Ridgway, S.H. and R.J. Harrison (eds.). 1981. *Handbook of Marine Mammals: Vol. 1, The Walrus, Sea Lions, Fur Seals and Sea Otter*. Academic Press, London. 235pp.

Ridgway, S.H. and R.J. Harrison (eds.). 1981. *Handbook of Marine Mammals: Vol. 2, Seals*. Academic Press, London. 359pp.

Ridgway, S.H. and R.J. Harrison (eds.). 1985. *Handbook of Marine Mammals: Vol. 3, Sirenians and Baleen Whales*. Academic Press, London. 362pp.

Ridgway, S.H. and R.J. Harrison (eds.). 1989. *Handbook of Marine Mammals: Vol. 4, River Dolphins and the Larger Toothed Whales*. Academic Press, London. 362pp.

Ridgway, S.H. and R.J. Harrison (eds.). 1994. *Handbook of Marine Mammals: Vol. 5, The First Book of Dolphins*. Academic Press, London. 416pp.

Ridgway, S.H. and R.J. Harrison (eds.). 1999. *Handbook of Marine Mammals: Vol. 6, Second Book of Dolphins and Porpoises*. Academic Press, London. 486pp.

Waring, G.T., D.L. Palka, K.D. Mullin, J.H.W. Hain, L.J. Hansen, and K.D. Bisack. 1997. *U.S. Atlantic and Gulf of Mexico Marine Mammal Stock Assessments*. NOAA Technical Memo NMFS-NE-114. Department of Commerce, NOAA/NMFS/NEFSC, Woods Hole, Mass. 250pp.

Wynne, K. 2012. *Guide to Marine Mammals of Alaska*, 4th edn. Alaska Sea Grant College Program, University of Alaska Fairbanks, Fairbanks, Alaska. 75pp.

Sea Turtles:

Bjorndal, K.A. (ed.). 1995. *Biology and Conservation of Sea Turtles,* revised edition. Smithsonian Institution Press, Washington, D.C. 615pp.

Ernst, C.H. and R.W. Barbour. 1989. *Turtles of the World.* Smithsonian Institution Press, Washington, D.C. 313pp.

Lutz, P.L. and J.A. Musick. 1997. *The Biology of Sea Turtles.* CRC Press, Boca Raton, Fla. 432pp.

Musick, J.A. 1988. *The Sea Turtles of Virginia with Notes on Identification and Natural History,* second revised edition. Virginia Sea Grant College Program, Virginia Institute of Marine Science, Gloucester Point, Va. 22pp.

National Marine Fisheries Service and U.S. Fish and Wildlife Service. 1991. *Recovery Plan for U.S. Population of Atlantic Green Turtle.* National Marine Fisheries Service, Washington, D.C. 52pp.

National Marine Fisheries Service and U.S. Fish and Wildlife Service. 1991. *Recovery Plan for U.S. Population of Loggerhead Turtle.* National Marine Fisheries Service, Washington, D.C. 64pp.

National Marine Fisheries Service and U.S. Fish and Wildlife Service. 1992. *Recovery Plan for Leatherback Turtles in the U.S. Caribbean, Atlantic, and Gulf of Mexico.* National Marine Fisheries Service, Washington, D.C. 52pp.

National Marine Fisheries Service and U.S. Fish and Wildlife Service. 1993. *Recovery Plan for Hawksbill Turtles in the U.S. Caribbean Sea, Atlantic Ocean, and Gulf of Mexico.* National Marine Fisheries Service, St. Petersburg, Fla. 52pp.

National Marine Fisheries Service and U.S. Fish and Wildlife Service. 1995. *Status Reviews of Sea Turtles Listed Under the Endangered Species Act of 1973.* National Marine Fisheries Service, Silver Spring, Md. 139pp.

National Research Council. 1990. *Decline of the Sea Turtles: Causes and Prevention.* National Academy Press, Washington, D.C. 259pp.

Shoop, C.R. and R.D. Kenney. 1992. Seasonal distributions and abundances of loggerhead and leatherback sea turtles in waters of the northeastern United States. *Herpetological Monographs* 6:43–67.

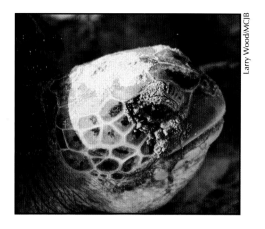

Larry Wood/MCJB

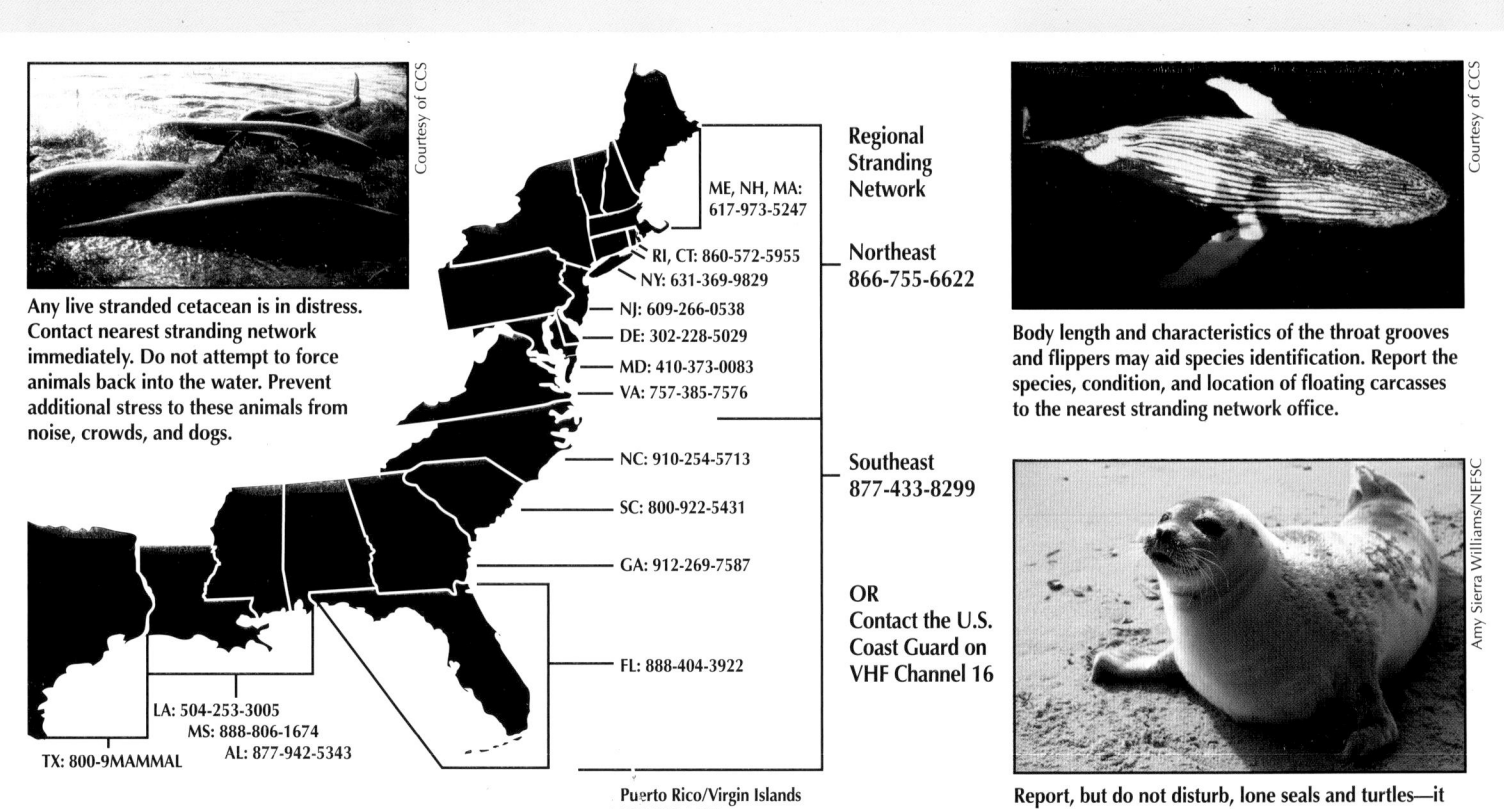

Courtesy of CCS

Any live stranded cetacean is in distress. Contact nearest stranding network immediately. Do not attempt to force animals back into the water. Prevent additional stress to these animals from noise, crowds, and dogs.

ME, NH, MA:
617-973-5247

RI, CT: 860-572-5955
NY: 631-369-9829

NJ: 609-266-0538
DE: 302-228-5029
MD: 410-373-0083
VA: 757-385-7576

NC: 910-254-5713

SC: 800-922-5431

GA: 912-269-7587

FL: 888-404-3922

LA: 504-253-3005
MS: 888-806-1674
AL: 877-942-5343

TX: 800-9MAMMAL

Regional
Stranding
Network

Northeast
866-755-6622

Southeast
877-433-8299

OR
Contact the U.S.
Coast Guard on
VHF Channel 16

Puerto Rico/Virgin Islands
787-538-4684

Or go to www.nmfs.noaa.gov/pr/health/networks.htm

Courtesy of CCS

Body length and characteristics of the throat grooves and flippers may aid species identification. Report the species, condition, and location of floating carcasses to the nearest stranding network office.

Amy Sierra Williams/NEFSC

Report, but do not disturb, lone seals and turtles—it can endanger both you and them.